MW00846873

ARIZONA STATE PARKS

Arizona State Parks

A Guide to Amazing Places in the Grand Canyon State

ROGER NAYLOR

Roger Naylor

University of New Mexico Press • Albuquerque

Library of Congress Cataloging-
in-Publication Data

Names
Naylor, Roger, 1957– author.
Title
Arizona state parks: a guide to amazing
places in the Grand Canyon State /
Roger Naylor.
Description
Albuquerque: University of New Mexico
Press, 2019. | Series: Southwest adventure
series | Includes bibliographical references
and index. |
Identifiers
LCCN 2019000974 (print)
LCCN 2019001516 (e-book)
ISBN 9780826359292 (e-book)
ISBN 9780826359285 (pbk.: alk. paper)
Subjects
LCSH: Parks—Arizona—Guidebooks.
Classification
LCC F809.3 (e-book)
LCC F809.3. N39 2019 (print)
DDC 917.9104—dc23

LC record available at https://lccn.loc.gov
/2019000974

Cover photo: Brittlebush blooms along the
trails at Lost Dutchman State Park.
Photo by the author.
Frontispiece: Catalina State Park. Courtesy
of Rick Mortensen.
Table of Contents Photo: Lake Havasu State
Park. Courtesy of Arizona State Parks
and Trails.

All maps by Mindy Basinger Hill

Composed in Minion Pro and Gotham

TO MARSHALL TRIMBLE, DOLAN ELLIS,

BOB BOZE BELL, AND ANGEL DELGADILLO

Four men who made Arizona—and the world—

a better and more interesting place.

Contents

Illustrations

Arizona
State Parks

ARIZONA STATE PARKS MILEAGE CHART

PARKS	PHOENIX	TUSCON	FLAGSTAFF
Alamo Lake	136	275	244
Boyce Thompson Arboretum	68	105	204
Buckskin Mountain	147	287	234
Catalina	110	16	258
Cattail Cove	151	301	223
Colorado River	186	239	322
Dead Horse Ranch	104	218	70
Fool Hollow Lake	176	189	140
Fort Verde	90	204	57
Granite Mountain Hotshots	88	204	131
Homolovi	201	329	72
Jerome	111	225	76
Kartchner Caverns	161	50	309
Lake Havasu	202	317	206
Lost Dutchman	42	137	182
Lyman Lake	221	246	158
McFarland	64	78	210
Oracle	118	36	275
Patagonia Lake	175	82	336
Picacho Peak	68	40	219
Red Rock	117	231	38
Riordan Mansion	143	257	1
River Island	148	288	233
Roper Lake	173	124	306
Slide Rock	115	236	23
Tombstone Courthouse	185	71	328
Tonto Natural Bridge	105	201	106
Tubac Presidio	158	45	301
Yuma Territorial Prison	185	238	321

AMENITIES IN ALL ARIZONA STATE PARKS

PARKS	BOATING	CABINS	CAMPING	FISHING	HIKING	HISTORIC BUILDINGS	MOUNTAIN BIKING	PICNIC AREAS	PROGRAMS	SWIMMING
Alamo Lake	•	•	•	•				•		•
Boyce Thompson Arboretum			•	•				•	•	
Buckskin Mountain	•		•	•	•			•	•	•
Catalina		•	•		•			•	•	•
Cattail Cove	•	•	•	•				•	•	•
Colorado River						•	•			
Dead Horse Ranch	•	•	•	•	•		•	•	•	•
Fool Hollow Lake	•		•	•	•			•	•	•
Fort Verde						•		•	•	
Granite Mountain Hotshots						•				
Homolovi			•		•			•	•	
Jerome						•		•		
Kartchner Caverns		•	•		•			•	•	
Lake Havasu	•		•	•	•			•	•	•
Lost Dutchman	•	•		•				•	•	•
Lyman Lake	•	•	•	•	•			•		
McFarland						•		•		
Oracle					•	•	•	•	•	
Patagonia Lake	•	•	•	•	•			•		•
Picacho Peak			•		•				•	
Red Rock					•	•	•	•	•	•
Riordan Mansion						•	•		•	
River Island	•		•	•	•			•		•
Roper Lake	•	•	•	•	•			•		•
Slide Rock					•	•		•	•	•
Tombstone Courthouse						•		•	•	
Tonto Natural Bridge					•	•		•		•
Tubac Presidio					•	•		•	•	
Yuma Territorial Prison						•		•	•	

Introduction

Coyote paid me no mind.

He was just going about coyote business when he crossed the trail 50 yards ahead, giving me a sideways glance and tongue wag, which is canine for "what up?" I watched as he loped across a meadow sprinkled with blackfoot daisies. The clumps of white flowers were scattered about like discarded wedding bouquets. Maybe a herd of runaway brides had stampeded past.

The low slant of morning sun bathed the landscape in a creamy, dreamy light. A faint fragrance danced in on the breeze—the unmistakable and haunting perfume of moisture-kissed creosote. Somewhere rain was falling. Darkly bruised clouds shoved each other around above the red cliffs of Sedona some 15 miles across the valley. Hopefully, the storm would move this way. Until then I enjoyed my sunshine and solitude. I was alone in a place quiet enough to hear the crunch of coyote paws as my new amigo trotted toward distant hills. It was just a typical day in small-town Arizona.

Some folks head for the treadmills at the gym or a track at a local school. Others may enjoy a brisk constitutional through their neighborhood. But I prefer to take my walks into the outback, courtesy of Arizona State Parks and Trails. Dead Horse Ranch State Park sits along the banks of the Verde River minutes from my house. And just that quickly I can escape. I tumble off the grid whenever I feel the urge. Instant access to wild country becomes a rare and wonderful gift. Dead Horse Ranch is a place where I get to experience broad scenic vistas, animal encounters, wildflower sightings, a sky full of drama, river, forest, and mountain all in the span of a simple morning hike.

While I have always enjoyed exploring the state parks of Arizona, I cherish them even more after moving in just down the road from one. I began to understand the quality-of-life benefits they provide for residents and the desirable destinations they are for travelers.

Arizona is best known for a national park. This is, after all, the Grand Canyon State. It's pretty sweet, having one of the Seven Natural Wonders of the World entirely within our borders. But as exotic and amazing as that is, we are defined by something more intimate—the hidden treasures of Arizona State Parks and Trails.

The entire story of Arizona can be told through its 35 state parks and natural areas. The staggering diversity of the landscape is revealed—classic Sonoran

Desert, high grasslands, craggy canyons, mountain forests, fragile riparian corridors, and a playground of lakes and rivers.

Some of Arizona's best spring wildflower displays take place in the parks (Lost Dutchman, Picacho Peak, and Catalina). The pristine underground cavern voted the best cave in the nation (Kartchner Caverns), the world's largest travertine natural bridge (Tonto Natural Bridge), and one of the Southwest's most legendary swimming holes (Slide Rock) are all in state parks.

The history of Arizona unfolds across the state parks. There are parks that preserve the prehistoric dwellings of Native people (Homolovi), a Spanish Colonial–era presidio (Tubac Presidio), an Indian Wars–era fort (Fort Verde), a Civil War battlefield (Picacho Peak), a Wild West courthouse (Tombstone Courthouse), and a notorious hoosegow (Yuma Territorial Prison). The foundations of Arizona's early economy—mining, ranching, and timber (Jerome, Oracle, and Riordan Mansion)—are all represented by the parks.

Despite the fact that we are an arid state, you could never prove it by spending time at the parks, which include an abundance of water, such as high-mountain lakes (Fool Hollow Lake and Lyman Lake) and a surprising collection of lowland-desert fishing holes and swimming holes (Alamo Lake, Patagonia Lake, Roper Lake, and Dankworth Pond). Perhaps most intriguing of all, Arizona's enticing West Coast, defined by the mighty Colorado River, is absolutely packed with parks along its most scenic stretches (Buckskin Mountain, River Island, Cattail Cove, and Lake Havasu.)

The state parks provide the same kind of experience found in national parks and monuments, except that it feels more intimate, less hurried. Nearly every park offers some combination of guided hikes, nature talks, presentations, concerts, star parties, and other events. You have a chance to explore a new region, learn something, have an adventure, and still be back home before the weekend is over.

In 2017 I visited every Arizona state park. It seemed like a good idea. The parks were turning 60, I was turning 60—it felt like kismet. And as an Arizona travel writer, poking around in every nook and cranny of this amazing state is part of the job description. It ended up being a very good year, at least for the parks (I think they're aging better than me). The parks experienced all-time highs in attendance and revenue. And to cap the year off in fairy-tale fashion, they were acknowledged as the very best in the nation at what they do.

In September 2017 Arizona State Parks and Trails received the Gold Medal Award from the American Academy for Park and Recreation Administration. The prestigious accolade honored their excellence in long-range planning, resource management, and innovative approaches to delivering superb park and recreation services.

The author enjoys a late-winter hike on the trails of Dead Horse Ranch State Park.
Courtesy of Rick Mortensen, Cincinnati.

The award capped a remarkable transformation for Arizona State Parks and Trails. The agency that was founded in 1957 teetered on the brink of ruin just a few years ago. A state budget crisis in 2009 triggered legislative sweeps of parks-department funds, depriving them of millions of dollars. Several parks were closed; others had their hours slashed. The agency faced an overwhelming deficit.

Fortunately, dire circumstances prompted action. While national parks are often in remote settings, most Arizona state parks are part of a community. These are vital economic engines for small towns. Partnerships were forged with local governments and nonprofits to keep the gates open and the lights on at many of the parks. An army of volunteers stepped forward and went to work. The parks survived the crisis. Yet simply surviving wasn't enough. Changes needed to be made if the agency was going to thrive.

The leadership team of Arizona State Parks and Trails established a self-sufficient funding structure and implemented a plan to reinvest in the system. The agency was streamlined and began working across the jurisdictions of other recreation and conservation agencies, dramatically expanding park outreach.

Today the parks receive no general-fund money yet have begun producing a steady revenue stream. All parks that closed have reopened. And the roster continues to expand. The very poignant Granite Mountain Hotshots Memorial State Park was added in November 2016. Look for the two newest—Havasu Riviera State Park on Arizona's West Coast and Rockin' River Ranch State Park, nestled on the banks of the Verde River—to open in 2019 or 2020.

Winning the Gold Medal Award simply validated what Arizona residents have known for years—it is a park system without peer. State parks exhibit a treasure trove of natural and cultural wonders. They deliver wild country almost right to our doorsteps. They are bite-size, family-friendly adventures.

With this book I try to provide all the information you need before venturing out to explore Arizona's state parks. Of course, hours, fees, and facilities are subject to change. It's always a good idea to call ahead or visit the website for the most current information. That's also how you'll learn about any activities, programs, or events scheduled that might be of interest.

In addition to park details, I provide information about the communities where they're located. With each park I include several nearby attractions such as museums, jeep tours, walking tours, historic sites, ghost towns, scenic drives, wineries, and more. While you're in the area, you might as well experience all the fun stuff you can. Those are key elements of a good road trip. And at its very core, this book is a bible of Arizona road trips.

Imagine this scenario: Take a year and visit every single award-winning state park in Arizona. Explore the far corners of this astonishing, astounding state. Reconnect to the small towns, the rugged scenery, and the curving two-lane roads. Hike, fish, swim, camp, stargaze, and learn. Do all the things you yearn to do but so rarely find the time for.

Play hard. Live deliberately. Get healthy. Breathe.

Now *that's* a gold medal year by anyone's standards. I know it was for me.

Arizona State Parks and Trails

Arizona State Parks and Trails manages 35 parks and natural areas. Of those, 32 are currently open to the public. Two more are scheduled to open soon.

Park Headquarters

Visitors can pick up free information, purchase passes, shop for merchandise, make camping reservations, renew fishing licenses, and receive trip-planning assistance at the Arizona State Parks Outdoor Recreation Information Center.

The facility is located at 23751 North 23rd Avenue, Suite 190, Phoenix, Arizona. It's just off Interstate 17 at the Pinnacle Peak Road exit.

Operating Hours

Arizona State Parks are open year-round. Some park museums' and contact stations' hours may fluctuate seasonally. For specific park schedules, go to azstateparks.com or call 877-MY-PARKS (877-697-2757).

Entrance Fees

Some parks are free to enter. At most parks, day-use fees range from $5 to $30 seasonally for adults. The entrance-fee key used in this book is as follows:

$ = $10 and under
$$ = $11 to $20
$$$ = $21 to $30

Park Passes

Annual passes are available—and they are a bargain. The Standard Annual Pass allows day-use access at almost all Arizona state parks for the pass holder and up to three additional adults in the same vehicle. The only exceptions are weekends and holidays from April 1 through October 31 at Lake Havasu, Cattail Cove, River Island, Buckskin Mountain, Patagonia Lake, and Slide Rock. The pass is also not accepted for entry at Boyce Thompson Arboretum and Kartchner Caverns.

The Premium Annual Pass allows the pass holder and up to three adults in the same vehicle access to all parks at anytime, except Boyce Thompson and Kartchner Caverns. However, if you are taking a cave tour or camping at Kartchner Caverns, the entry fee is waived.

Passes are for day use only and do not apply to fees for things like camping and certain guided tours.

The Military Discount Program provides a 50 percent day-use discount to active duty, guard, and reserve military, as well as Arizona-resident retired military and disabled military veterans. Arizona-residents who are 100 percent-disabled military veterans receive a free pass. Please bring all necessary documentation when applying for passes. Discounts include pass holder and up to three additional adults in the same vehicle.

Accessibility

All Arizona state parks provide access to parking areas, visitor centers, restrooms, and picnic ramadas. Several parks include additional wheelchair-friendly facilities, such as trails, cabins, campsites, showers, and fishing docks. Kartchner Caverns is one of the extremely rare wheelchair-accessible caves in the world.

Arizona State Parks and Trails has a dedicated Americans with Disabilities Act (ADA) coordinator on staff who works to catalog and improve accessibility at all of the parks. The goal is to make as much of the parks available as possible to those with disabilities.

Pets

Most Arizona state parks welcome pets. Animals must be kept on a leash at all times and owners are expected to clean up after them. With the exception of service animals, pets are not allowed in historic buildings or museums, on developed beaches, or at other environmentally sensitive areas.

Pets are not allowed at Red Rock, near the swim area at Slide Rock, on the trails at Tonto Natural Bridge, in the cave at Kartchner Caverns, or in the Bighorn Management Areas in Catalina.

Camping

Almost half of the parks allow for overnight stays. Campgrounds include sites for RVs and tents as well as camping cabins. Many campsites offer electric (30 amp and 50 amp) and water hookups. Restrooms and showers are located in the campgrounds. All camping parks offer reservations online or by phone; other campsites are available on a first-come, first-serve basis. Several parks offer group camping sites. Reservations can be made online or by calling 877-MY-PARKS.

Patagonia Lake and Cattail Cove offer campsites accessible only by boat. Sonoita Creek Natural Area contains primitive backpacking campsites.

For folks who like to rough it in comfort, select parks offer camping cabins. The rustic wooden cabins are furnished with beds, a table, chairs, a ceiling fan, electricity, heating, and air conditioning. Visitors must provide their own linen. Cabins feature a porch and include a picnic table and barbecue grill. At least one ADA-accessible cabin is available in each park that offers cabins. Reservations can be made online or by calling 877-MY-PARKS.

Arizona Family Campout Program

Ever wanted to take the family camping but don't know where to start? The Arizona Family Campout Program makes it easy. Designed for those with little or no camping experience, the program allows families to spend a night in the great outdoors, no wilderness skills required.

During a weekend packed with activities, families will be introduced to new adventures at parks across the state. Campers will learn how to set up a tent, build a fire, and cook outside. Activities vary from park to park but may include guided hikes, archery, geocaching, fishing, live-animal demonstrations, mountain-bike clinics, geology presentations, birding, astronomy, and campfire stories. Families will also get to work on a service project such as tree planting.

The program provides tents, sleeping mats, camp chairs, lanterns, flashlights, first-aid kits, and all activity equipment. They will also supply water, coffee, tea, sports drinks, campfire treats, and a Dutch-oven dinner dessert. Families just need to bring sleeping bags (or other bedding), pillows, water bottles, personal items, and food for two lunches, dinner, and breakfast. Children 5 years and younger and pets cannot attend this program. Since this is to learn about tent camping, RVs are not allowed. Check the website for dates and more details.

Natural Areas

Natural Areas are portions of land that have scientific, educational, and aesthetic value by reason of distinctive natural features. In Arizona, natural areas have as their primary purpose the protection and preservation of the site's natural resources.

Arizona State Parks and Trails is responsible for three designated State Natural Areas (SNAs): Sonoita Creek, Verde River Greenway, and San Rafael Ranch.

Sonoita Creek SNA is located downstream from Patagonia Lake State Park along lower Sonoita Creek. The area supports uncommon plant species and a high diversity of birds and other species. The federally protected endangered Gila topminnow, a rare native fish, thrives in perennial Sonoita Creek and its tributaries. Find more information on Sonoita Creek SNA in the Patagonia Lake State Park chapter.

Verde River Greenway SNA is a critical portion of the river based on its rich natural and cultural resources as well as on a growing demand for recreational use. It is located next to Dead Horse Ranch State Park. Recognizing the need to protect this rare habitat, the Arizona State Parks Board has continued to acquire land along the Verde River as money and opportunities become available. Find more information on Verde River Greenway SNA in the Dead Horse Ranch State Park chapter.

San Rafael SNA preserves one of the finest native grasslands in the state. The grasslands of this sweeping valley in southeastern Arizona are especially rare because they have not suffered an encroachment of cacti, shrubs, and exotic plant species. This ranch was once a Mexican land grant. At this time there are no plans to open the park to the public.

Arizona Premier Trails System

Arizona State Parks and Trails has begun the almost impossible task of selecting trails for the Arizona Premier Trails System. They teamed up with the Arizona State Committee on Trails to recognize the most beautiful, most exciting, and most historically significant trails across the state. Each trail nominated goes through a comprehensive selection process and must meet specific criteria in various categories.

The Arizona Premier Trails System will eventually include up to 100 of the best nonmotorized trails, such as hiking, biking, equestrian, river, and riparian trails. This diverse list will inspire people to experience even more of the backcountry wonders and cultural history that are all part of the Arizona story.

There is a current list of Arizona Premier Trails on the website.

Volunteer in the Parks

Volunteers are a vital component of Arizona State Parks and Trails. Those who would like to donate their time and talents will find ample opportunities to make an impact. Volunteers often lead hikes and discussions, give tours, participate in living-history programs, act as site stewards and campground hosts, and help with routine maintenance. If you live near a park, it's easy. But you can also make a big difference with a one-time project. Call or visit the website for more information on volunteer opportunities.

Northern Arizona State Parks

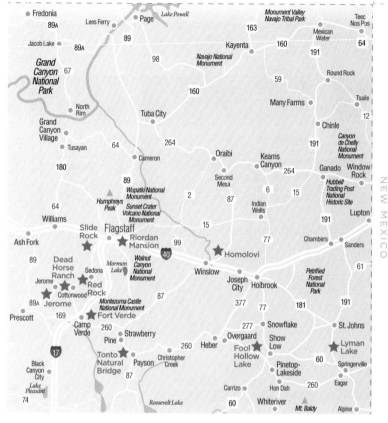

AMENITIES IN NORTHERN ARIZONA STATE PARKS

PARKS	Tonto Natural Bridge	Slide Rock	Riordan Mansion	Red Rock	Lyman Lake	Jerome	Homolovi	Fort Verde	Fool Hollow Lake	Dead Horse Ranch
BOATING					•				•	•
CABINS					•				•	
CAMPING					•		•		•	•
FISHING					•				•	•
HIKING	•	•		•	•		•			•
HISTORIC BUILDINGS		•	•	•		•	•	•		•
MOUNTAIN BIKING				•						
PICNIC AREAS	•	•	•	•	•		•		•	•
PROGRAMS	•	•	•	•		•	•		•	•
SWIMMING		•		•	•				•	

The reflection of rocky cliffs is captured in the Dead Horse Ranch lagoon. Courtesy of Rick Mortensen, Cincinnati.

Dead Horse Ranch State Park and Verde River Greenway State Natural Area

Nearest Town: Cottonwood.

Why Go: Hikers, mountain bikers, anglers, kayakers, and birders will all have plenty to do at this recreation-intensive park and natural area, nestled on the banks of the Verde River.

The oddly named Dead Horse Ranch in Cottonwood is the most unsung state park in the system. Admittedly, I am biased since I live just minutes away and consider the property as an extension of my own backyard. But examine the amenities. It has everything you could want in a park.

Scenic campgrounds are complemented by camping cabins tucked down a shady lane. Picnic areas are plentiful. A pristine stretch of the Verde River winds through, perfect for kayakers, canoeists, anglers, swimmers, and kids that just want to splash around looking for frogs. A reedy marsh and sparkling lagoons increase the watery acreage and attract an amazing roster of birds and wildlife.

Hikers, mountain bikers, and equestrians enjoy over 20 miles of trails. Despite the name, Dead Horse is a great place to fork a saddle. If you don't have your own bronc, no worries. A concessionaire offers wrangler-guided trail rides.

See what I mean? It's a terrific park by any standard.

The ancient pueblo of Tuzigoot is visible from Lower Raptor Trail.
Courtesy of Rick Mortensen, Cincinnati.

Kids Say the Darndest Things

Maybe it's the name that scares some folks away. Not that the park is empty. On the contrary, it's pretty bustling for much of the year, and the campgrounds are packed in spring and fall. But it does fly under the radar a bit for the general public. At first glance, the name doesn't give you much information about the park. Yet it sort of does.

In the late 1940s the Ireys family looked at ranches in Cottonwood, including one with an equine carcass. When the father asked which property they liked, the kids said, "The one with the dead horse." The name stuck. In 1973 when they sold the land to Arizona State Parks, the Ireys made retaining the name a condition of the sale.

So it started as a family ranch, and after all these years it still retains that welcoming feel. Dead Horse Ranch is a huge part of the community. I think that's true of all state parks located in or near small towns. In almost every case they preserve a vital piece of history or a slice of dramatic scenery that is crucial to that town's identity.

What the Dead Horse moniker doesn't do is give you an accurate sense of the pervasive serenity and striking beauty of this park. Nestled in the Verde Valley, the park stretches along the river and across the rolling limestone hills in the shadow of a wall of mountains. The Black Hills, topped by the bulk of Mingus Mountain, frame the valley. The former mining town of Jerome can be seen clinging halfway up the steep slope.

An angler tries his luck at one of three Dead Horse Ranch lagoons. Courtesy of Arizona State Parks and Trails, Phoenix.

Fast Fact: Located within the Prescott National Forest, Mingus Mountain rises to an elevation of 7,818 feet. Mingus serves as a popular launch site for hang gliders.

A River Runs through It

More than just lovely, this is an exceedingly rare stretch of river flowing through the park. The Verde River Greenway State Natural Area is a separately managed unit of Dead Horse and protects almost 1,000 acres of riparian and upland habitat. When first designated, it sheltered 6 river miles, but it continues to grow and today encompasses 35 river miles.

The greenway consists of a Fremont cottonwood / Goodding's willow riparian

forest, one of 20 such stands left in the world. The goal is to maintain this fragile and vital habitat in a natural state. A wide range of birds and wildlife rely on it. Deer, coyotes, beaver, raccoons, bobcats, and the occasional mountain lion can be seen here. Additionally, the river supports nearly 20 threatened or endangered species including river otter, southwestern bald eagles, and lowland leopard frogs.

For an up-close look, take the Verde River Greenway Trail, meandering among the trees near the water's edge. Popular with birders, this 2-mile level, sandy path passes through groves of massive cottonwoods and some of the best nesting habitat in the area.

Water and trails are what define Dead Horse. This is likely the most extensive network of hiking, biking, and equestrian trails in the state park system. And they can be enjoyed by almost anyone.

Hiking the Soft Backcountry

The Canopy Trail is a quarter-mile ADA-accessible path looping through the cottonwood shade. It gives visitors with limited mobility an opportunity to enjoy bird-watching and wildlife viewing away from the pavement.

Likewise, the paths around the lagoons provide easy access to beautiful scenery. A trail circles each (West Lagoon 0.39 miles, Middle Lagoon 0.41 miles, and East Lagoon 0.72 miles), and the firm, crushed-granite surface makes it a popular outing for hikers, anglers, dog walkers, and folks in wheelchairs. These paths make a splendid oasis lined with shade trees, benches, and small fishing piers.

This is one of my favorite Arizona places. When I stop at Dead Horse for a hike, I almost always pay a visit to the lagoons before or after. Sometimes on lazy days the lagoons become my hike as I make multiple laps, enjoying the antics of ducks or great

Fast Fact: The park contains a small historic cemetery where miners, cowboys, and Hispanic laborers are buried. The graveyard is owned and managed by the Trustees of the San Luis Rey Cemetery.

blue herons preening on the shore. Turtles sun themselves on partially submerged logs, and a rowdy chorus of redwing blackbirds gossips in the cattails.

Several other short trails crisscross the park interior, including 1-mile Mesa Trail that circles the top of the hill above the Red-Tail Hawk Campground. The trail to Tavasci Marsh follows an old road through a mesquite bosque that ends at a viewing platform overlooking a reed-choked marsh, which is a bit of a treat. As an arid state, Arizona is not known for an abundance of marshes. It's also been my experience that this trail teems with wildlife.

For the heart of the Dead Horse hiking and mountain-biking experience, ramble into the soft backcountry. The limestone hills above the river are dotted with creosote, juniper, and twisted crucifixion thorn. You can start from either Lime Kiln Trail or Lower Raptor Trail. You'll enjoy views of Mingus Mountain and the red rocks of Sedona across the valley. If you crave a closer look at the crimson cliffs, just continue on the Lime Kiln. It leaves the park, tracing the route of an old wagon road for 15 miles until it ends on the doorstep of Red Rock State Park in Sedona.

Both Lime Kiln and Lower Raptor connect with other trails, some that exit the park and continue across the national forest. The variety of routes available, including some excellent long-distance outings, is why Dead Horse Ranch State Park is loved by mountain bikers and hikers like me who appreciate having a backyard that stretches to a distant horizon.

The Verde River provides excellent birding habitat. Courtesy of Arizona State Parks and Trails, Phoenix.

When You Go

Dead Horse Ranch State Park is located in Cottonwood at 675 Dead Horse Ranch Road, 928-634-5283, azstateparks.com.

Admission

$ per vehicle (up to four adults).

Boating

Nonmotorized watercraft (oar power only, no sails) are allowed in the lower lagoons. Boating is not permitted in the upper (west) lagoon. A launch ramp and dock are available at the east lagoon. Children 12 and under are required to wear a personal flotation device at all times when boating.

The Verde River is a popular destination for kayakers and canoeists. A river access point is located upstream at the bridge below Tuzigoot National Monument. You can put in at the Tuzigoot Bridge and take out at Dead Horse, or put in at Dead Horse and take out at 89A at the Bridgeport Bridge. There are lots of twists, turns, and channels, so do some research beforehand. Paddle maps are available on the website for all of the Verde River Greenway.

Cabins

Dead Horse Ranch features eight heated, air-conditioned cabins, each with a full-sized bed, a bunk bed, a table, chairs, and a covered wooden porch. Bring your own bedding or sleeping bags, towels, utensils, and so on. And pack a flashlight for nighttime walks to the restrooms and showers.

Camping

There are more than 100 large RV sites. Most pull-through sites can accommodate 40-foot motor homes and truck and trailer rigs up to 65 feet and include potable water and electric. Generators are prohibited. Blackhawk Loop features 17 nonelectric sites reserved exclusively for tents. All campground loops include ADA-accessible restroom facilities and showers.

Events

The Verde Valley Birding and Nature Festival, one of the preeminent birding events in the state, takes place in April. The festival is held at the park but has expanded into diverse habitats across the Verde Valley, through a series of guided field trips and workshops. Featured speakers, dozens of vendors, and educational programs cater to nature enthusiasts of all ages.

In September, celebrate the river and bid adios to summer. Verde River Day promotes preservation of this special habitat through informative exhibits, guided bird walks, and live-animal demonstrations. A rock-climbing wall, sand-castle-building contests, and canoe and kayak races are just a few of the fun activities to go along with the food booths and live entertainment.

Cottonwood celebrates Historic Arizona 89A with their Walkin' on Main event. The segment of 89A stretching from Jerome through Cottonwood is one of only three highways recognized by Arizona as an official Historic Road. Spend a fall day enjoying live music, a display of classic cars, a juried art show, and an outdoor wine-tasting event. It takes place in November in Old Town Cottonwood, a picturesque collection of historic buildings dating back to the 1920s and '30s.

Fishing

The park offers great fishing opportunities for beginners and more experienced anglers alike. The river and lagoons are stocked with rainbow trout throughout the winter. The lagoons are stocked with channel catfish in the warmer season. Fish species include largemouth bass, catfish, bluegill, crappie, and trout. Fly-fishing the river and lagoons is becoming increasingly popular. A valid Arizona fishing license is required for anglers 10 years and older.

Horseback Rides

Dead Horse Ranch includes an equestrian concessionaire. Trail Horse Adventures leads outings of 60 minutes, 90 minutes, and longer. Take a leisurely ride through the park, along the river, and even have a picnic lunch. 928-634-5276, trailhorse adventures.com.

Picnic Areas

Strategically placed picnic tables are located throughout the park, in day-use areas and campgrounds, and around the lagoons. Many ramadas also include ADA-accessible picnic tables.

Swimming

Swimming is allowed anywhere along the river. There is no lifeguard on duty, so all water-based activities are at your own risk. Swimming is not permitted in the lagoons.

Trails

Over 20 miles of mixed-use trails crisscross the park and extend into the surrounding national forest. The centerpiece route is a partial loop formed by Lime Kiln, Thumper, and Lower Raptor, a bit over 7 miles that travels through hilly terrain and crosses open meadows. Hikers and equestrians should travel counterclockwise while mountain bikers will enjoy it more by riding clockwise. Another great option is to combine Lower Raptor and Bones Trail for a 7-mile loop full of long, sinuous curves as it crosses rolling hills slashed by shallow canyons with great mountain views. A personal favorite.

Nearby Attractions

Located between Clarkdale and Cottonwood and visible from Dead Horse, the ruins of an ancient Sinagua pueblo crown a hilltop overlooking the Verde River. Tuzigoot National Monument protects the remains of a terraced 110-room village with wraparound views. The National Park Service has restored one of the two-story structures so visitors can admire the building techniques and materials used by these resourceful people. 928-634-5564, www.nps.gov/tuzi.

Alcohol has always played a role in the fortunes of Cottonwood. During Prohibition this was a bootlegging hotspot. Today the wine industry is fueling the drive, with family-owned vineyards growing on fertile hillsides, multiple tasting rooms, and eager chefs pairing a great meal with the local vino. The Verde Valley Wine Trail helps you track them all down and plan a great getaway for lovers of food and drink. Cheers! www.vvwinetrail.com.

The small Clemenceau Heritage Museum occupies the former classrooms of the old school building dating back to 1924. Clemenceau was formerly a company town founded by a mine owner to house workers for his nearby smelter. The museum displays artifacts and photographs that reflect the impact that mining, ranching, and farming had on the community. The Model Train Room combines history and cool toys. After the mines played out, Clemenceau was incorporated into Cottonwood. 1 North Willard Street, 928-634-2868, www.clemenceaumuseum.com.

Fool Hollow Lake Recreation Area

Nearest Town: Show Low.
Why Go: A sprawling high-country lake in the midst of a pine forest makes an enticing getaway for anglers, boaters, campers, and anyone needing a back-to-nature break.

It occurred to me as I walked along the edge of Fool Hollow Lake near the town of Show Low, a few miles from Deuce of Clubs Boulevard, that folks have a penchant for odd story-based names around these parts.

In 1879 Thomas Jefferson Adair moved into the area. Legend has it that his friends warned him only a fool would attempt to farm this rocky, thin-soiled basin. Instead of being dissuaded, Adair leaned into it, christening the place Fool Hollow.

Of course, Adair was only continuing a tradition. As the story goes, Marion Clark and Corydon Cooley homesteaded 100,000 acres in 1870. But a few years later, the men

Fast Fact: Show Low has continued its namesake tradition with a handful of tied city elections being determined by drawing for the deuce of clubs.

Fool Hollow Lake makes an enticing high-country getaway. Photo by the author.

had a falling out and decided to dissolve the partnership with a card game. They played a game called seven-up long into the night. A weary Clark finally told Cooley, "Show low and you take the ranch." Cooley turned over the two of clubs, winning the land and providing the name of the future town. The main drag through Show Low is named Deuce of Clubs.

Monsoon Morning

It was a bright summer morning in between storms when I strolled around 149-acre Fool Hollow Lake. Plenty of clouds lurked on the horizon, taking a breather after dumping two inches of rain the afternoon before. They looked fluffy and innocent and white as a snowman's navel, but I knew that was just a ruse.

During monsoon season, mornings are often luxuriously peaceful with plenty of fresh-scrubbed blue sky. But as the day wears on, clouds begin to gather in an angry cluster, shoving each other around. Skies darken, the wind howls, there's a clap of thunder, and suddenly you know that Bob Dylan was right all along: "a hard rain's a-gonna fall." Often the downpour ends as quickly as it began. The clouds break up but

promise to stay friends, and sun streams down again.

It makes us appreciate the calm mornings all the more. I followed the easy path that runs along the south and west sides of the lake. Anglers were out in force on the shore or on one of the half-dozen fishing platforms that extend into the water. Boats of varying sizes and shapes skimmed across the surface.

Fool Hollow is one of the most stunning lakes in the White Mountains, which is strong praise indeed. Over 40 scenic lakes adorn the high-country region in eastern Arizona, shimmering in meadows and forests, making this a popular summer getaway. But forget for a moment what Fool Hollow looks like in real life and study it on a map. There it is, a weird, gangly lake with watery branches spreading out in different directions. On paper it looks like a provocative inkblot in a Rorschach test—the kind a court-ordered psychiatrist would show you to help determine sentencing recommendations.

Maybe that's part of Fool Hollow's mystique. There's no vantage point in the park that allows you to see the entire lake. You discover it one vista at a time and it gives you a lot of different looks along the way. You see big open water but also several isolated coves, some quiet marshes, and long channels. This is the kind of lake that makes you want to jump in a kayak and go exploring.

Underwater Secrets

A dam was built in 1957 to corral the waters of Show Low Creek. The low-lying basin grew into a 149-acre lake ringed by ponderosa pines, a woodland mix of juniper and pinion pines, grassy pastures, and rocky cliffs.

The recreation area opened in 1994 as a result of an innovative four-way partnership between Arizona State Parks, the US

Forest Service, Arizona Game and Fish, and the City of Show Low. It's a pretty big deal. There really isn't another place like this in the state. The park sits at an elevation of 6,300 feet, surrounded by the Apache-Sitgreaves National Forest.

With abundant water and diverse habitats, Fool Hollow is a great spot for wildlife viewing. Keep an eye out for osprey, snowy egret, beaver, muskrat, bobcats, elk, and more. Black bears and mountain lions wander through. Bald eagles are winter visitors. Over the years, artificial islands were added to attract additional wildlife.

And more than just fish lurk beneath the quiet surface of the lake. An entire ghost town rests at the bottom.

Buried below the quiet waters are the remains of the small settlement known as Adair. The historic site consists of two housing foundations, the charred remains of a schoolhouse, various artifacts, and a few grave sites.

Butterfly Dance-Off

A hiking trail runs along part of the shoreline, dipping in and out of various habitats. There are plans to expand the trail to make

a complete loop around the water with a bridge crossing Show Low Creek, which would be pretty sweet.

Hiking in late July I saw wildflowers just starting to pop. The peak color looked to still be a couple of weeks away. Judging from the dense crop of plants with tight buds pushing through rocks and grass, a dazzling season was looming. Just one more benefit of the big rains that roll in one after another during an active monsoon season, officially designated in Arizona as June 15 through September 30.

The flowers may have just been starting, but an aerial ballet was in full swing. Dragonflies and damselflies were buzzing about—those little slivers of mobile color, those winged hyphens. A squadron of butterflies joined them. At this stage, it looked like the butterflies outnumbered the open blooms. I wondered if that sort of thing ever led to conflicts.

Do butterflies ever get territorial? I wouldn't be surprised. Cuteness has nothing to do with fierceness. I've seen enough hummingbirds the size of a nickel guarding a feeder as if it's their own personal moonshine still. But somehow it's hard to

Kayakers explore some of Fool Hollow Lake's sheltered coves.
Photo by the author.

imagine butterflies engaged in belligerent
behavior, throwing down in some wobbly,
fluttering dance-off. I started studying them
just in case this very thing was going on
right under my nose.

I stayed like that for a while. Couldn't tell
you how much time passed, but I realized
at some point that I was standing in a
meadow of flowers at the edge of a lake, at
the edge of a storm, listening to butterflies
beat back the breeze with their wings.

I can think of worse ways to spend a
summer day.

When You Go
Fool Hollow Lake Recreation Area is
located just outside Show Low off of Arizona 260 in the White Mountains of eastern Arizona. The entrance gate closes
nightly at 10:00 p.m. 928-537-3680,
azstateparks.com.

Admission
$ per vehicle (up to four adults).

Boating
Single-lane boat-launch ramps are available
on the east and west sides of the lake. Maximum of 10-horsepower gasoline engines
allowed.

Canoe, kayak, and paddleboard rentals
are available during summer through a
local concessionaire. J & T's Wild-Life Outdoors also offers mountain-bike rentals and
guided pontoon-boat tours. They're located
near the east boat-launch ramp. 928-892-
9170, www.jtwildlifeoutdoors.com.

Camping
There are 92 RV campsites with electric and
water service that can accommodate

40-foot rigs. The Mallard and Redhead
loops also have sewer available. There are 31
nonhookup sites.

Events
Ranger-led programs are conducted from
late May through early September and
range from educational talks at the Adair
Amphitheater to guided nature hikes and
children's programs.

Fishing
Fool Hollow Lake harbors a diverse population of fish species. Anglers can pursue
rainbow trout, largemouth and smallmouth
bass, black crappie, green sunfish, channel
catfish, walleye, and northern pike. There
are six fishing platforms around the lake
and two cleaning stations in the park. A
valid Arizona fishing license is required for
anglers 10 years and older.

Picnic Areas
Several picnic tables are spread along the
edge of the lake. There are also group sites
with restrooms, horseshoe pits, and play-
grounds.

Swimming
There is no designated swimming area so
make sure you swim near your boat or the
shore and in full view of others. Do not
swim near boat ramps, docks, or the dam.
The lake's temperature can vary from temperate in the shallows to near freezing in
open water. Swimmers should wear water
shoes to protect their feet from hazards. In
all situations, swimmers should exercise
caution. There is no lifeguard on duty, so
swimming is at your own risk.

Trails
A 1.5-mile walking trail runs along the
south and west sides of the lake. There are
plans to expand that trail to encircle the
entire lake and to build additional hiking

trails. Eventually, park rangers would like to connect their trail network to the White Mountain Trail System, which consists of over 200 miles of trails, designed as interconnected loops. They're found mostly in the forests surrounding Show Low and the neighboring communities of Pinetop and Lakeside. The system is built and maintained by TRACKS, a group of dedicated volunteers.

Nearby Attractions

The Show Low Museum was established in 1995 by five long-time residents looking for a place to put their stuff. It has since expanded to 16 rooms spread through two buildings. Themed rooms feature early families, old businesses, a blacksmith shop, post-office displays, and a jail. There is also a room dedicated to the 2002 Rodeo-Chediski Fire, which was the largest in Arizona history at the time. 561 East Deuce of Clubs Boulevard, 928-532-7115, www.showlowmuseum.wordpress.com.

The White Mountain Nature Center in Pinetop is a nonprofit educational organization that offers programs, information, and miles of hiking trails that fan out through meadows and forest crossing the Big Springs Environmental Study Area and circling Woodland Lake Park. It's a good spot for wildlife and wildflower sightings. Be sure to find out what programs they're offering during your visit. 425 South Woodland Road, 928-358-3069, whitemountainnaturecenter.org.

For those who prefer to ride rather than hike, Porter Mountain Stables in Lakeside will put you astride a gentle mount. Walk right out of the barn and into green meadows. Mosey through pine forest, crisscross a creek, and skirt the edge of a lake while scanning for wildlife. And that's just on the hour-long trail ride. They also offer two-hour and half-day rides, as well as a sunset outing. 3092 Jacks Road, 928-368-9599, www.portermtnstables.com.

Fort Verde State Historic Park

Nearest Town: Camp Verde.
Why Go: Experience life through the eyes of a frontier soldier at the best-preserved Apache Wars–era fort in Arizona.

Just a few generations ago, Arizona was the raggedy edge of the frontier. That began to change as mining camps exploded with each new find of ore, ranchers moved herds of cattle onto grassy plains, and settlers staked out prime farm acreage near rivers and streams.

The unrelenting migration pushed Native Americans from their lands and led to an upheaval of violence. The only thing that held the fragile territory together was a handful of army posts scattered from desert to mountains.

The army would establish a post as the need arose but many were quickly abandoned or reestablished elsewhere to deal with evolving threats. Despite their transitory nature, remnants of several forts have endured. One of the most intriguing of these is Fort Verde, displaying some of the oldest buildings in Arizona.

Fast Fact: Despite Hollywood depictions, army posts of the Old West were seldom imposing or elaborate. There were no stockade walls encircling a secure compound. Most forts in Arizona consisted of a few clustered buildings constructed out of whatever material was handy.

Original buildings still stand on Officer's Row at Fort Verde.
Courtesy of Mike Koopsen, Sedona.

The Army Marches In

For a place that's still standing after nearly 150 years, Fort Verde had a most inauspicious beginning. It was nearly done in by mosquitos and payroll problems.

In the mid-1800s, settlers moved into the Verde Valley, growing crops to sell to nearby miners and to folks in Prescott, the territorial capital. When the local Yavapais and Apaches were hungry, it seemed only natural for them to raid the farmers' crops.

The settlers requested military protection, and in August 1865, 20 soldiers were sent from Fort Whipple in Prescott, where they formed a small outpost to protect farms along West Clear Creek. A few months later, Captain H. S. Washburn arrived with Company E, 1st Arizona Volunteers. They established Camp Lincoln, north of the current site. But it was plagued by problems. The camp lacked supplies and the men were poorly fed and housed. Many refused to follow orders after months of not being paid. Disease ran rampant, and nearly half of the volunteers contracted malaria.

The first regular US troops arrived in September 1866. Order was restored and the post was renamed Camp Verde. But that too was short-lived. The site was abandoned in April 1871 when the new, and final, fort was constructed.

A Crook Takes Charge

That year famed Indian fighter Lieutenant Colonel George Crook was named commander of the Department of Arizona. He had waged successful campaigns against the Shoshones and Nez Percés and others in Oregon and California. Crook was a man who respected his adversaries and was always willing to negotiate, although a fierce and relentless fighter once the battle began.

"When they were pushed beyond endurance and would go on the warpath, we had to fight when our sympathies were with the Indians," Crook later wrote.

Crook believed it would take Apaches to find Apaches, so he implemented a program of Indian scouts. He paid his Native scouts the same as the white scouts. Many of his superiors were skeptical of the plan but it would prove to be decisive. Indian scouts from Fort Verde would go on to be awarded 11 Congressional Medals of Honor.

His next step was to build a military road tracing the high escarpment of the Mogollon Rim from Fort Apache in the eastern high country to Fort Verde and continuing on to Fort Whipple. This provided a more direct supply route, allowed quick access for forays into the Tonto Basin, and helped seal off escape for Apaches fleeing north.

The 236-mile route became one of the first major roads in Arizona. Decades later a portion of the old road was renovated by the Forest Service to become Forest Road 300. Better known as the Rim Road, this popular and still harrowing scenic drive leads backcountry enthusiasts to spectacular vistas and pristine camping.

Camp Verde served as a staging base for military operations in the surrounding countryside. Crook launched his campaign in November 1872, saturating the Tonto Basin with columns of troops and pursuing the Indians relentlessly during the winter months. As each band surrendered, it was relocated to a reservation. In 1873 Tonto Apache chief Chalipun and 300 of his followers traveled to Camp Verde to surrender to Crook on the porch of the commanding officer's quarters.

With the end of hostilities in the area, President Ulysses Grant promoted George Crook to brigadier general. He remained until 1874 in the Arizona territory, where he continued to build roads and repair forts, and he became an outspoken advocate for the humane treatment of Indians.

Fort for Sale

Camp Verde was renamed Fort Verde in 1878 to give it an air of permanence, but with the end of Indian raids the post was no longer needed. The last bugle sounded in 1891 as the troops pulled out. And eight years later the Department of Interior divided the site into small parcels and sold them at public auction.

The enlisted men's barracks were dismantled for lumber. A two-story adobe building on Officer's Row was converted to a barn. Some of the interior walls were removed to make room for livestock, causing the structure to collapse during a heavy snow. Yet four of the original buildings survived, occupied for decades as homes and apartments.

In the 1950s Camp Verde residents began working to preserve the remnants of the fort, which for a while served as a museum. Fort Verde State Historic Park was dedicated in 1970.

Holding Down the Fort

This is the best-preserved example of an Indian Wars–period fort in Arizona. Three buildings line Officer's Row: the living quarters for the commanding officer, the doctor's quarters, and the quarters for bachelor officers.

The buildings are constructed of adobe with walls as thick as 22 inches and have a French colonial design with a Mansard-style roof. This style disguises the second floor by extending the line of the roof down. The roofs are covered with cedar shingles.

Start at the visitor center for a quick orientation before beginning your tour. This was originally the fort's administration building and now serves as an informative museum containing exhibits on weaponry, uniforms, and the crucial role played by Indian scouts. Visitors can dress in period

---

Fast Fact: A bugle found on the Little Bighorn Battlefield where General George Custer and his men perished is on display at Fort Verde. This rare artifact was owned by a colonel later stationed at the fort.

Each building at Fort Verde serves as a museum. Photo by the author.

clothing available in the museum and have their family photos taken by the staff.

Each building has been converted to a museum-quality exhibit, furnished in the style of the times and stocked with original artifacts and memorabilia. Visitors who study the decor will gain an appreciation of life on the frontier for these soldiers: the hardships they faced and the comforts they sought. A glimpse at the crude surgical instruments displayed in the doctor's quarters will make everyone grateful for advancements in medical technology.

Living conditions were pretty bare bones in the bachelor officers' quarters, which were furnished with just what was needed to get by—cots, trunks, rifles, tables, and chairs. There's a communal kitchen in the rear of the building. The quarters were designed to have three bedrooms, and officers were often forced to share space. Army regulations stipulated one room and a kitchen for a lieutenant, two rooms and kitchen for a captain, and so on. But on the frontier, those regs were often ignored.

The commanding officer's quarters were much more plush and served as the center of social life at the fort. No doubt the CO's wife helped give it a homey touch. There are rugs, screens, ornate Victorian furniture, and even a china cabinet in the dining room. Upstairs bedrooms were used by the children. Their toys seem to be just where they left them.

Move slowly through the grounds. Notice the details. A scattering of picnic tables makes this a perfect spot to relax and unleash your imagination. A bugle rings throughout the day. If you listen closely, you might hear the faint echoes of whinnying horses and the rhythmic march of soldiers drilling on the parade grounds. Suddenly, it wasn't so long ago.

When You Go

Fort Verde State Historic Park is located at 125 East Hollamon Street in Fort Verde. The park is open daily from 9:00 a.m. to 5:00 p.m. 928-567-3275, azstateparks.com.

Admission

Adults and youths (7–13), $. Free admission for children 6 and under.

From 1873 to 1875 nearly 1,500 Indians from various tribes were placed on the Rio Verde Reservation with headquarters near present day Cottonwood. The Indians were assured that this would be their home as long as "the rivers run, the grass grows and hills endure." With the army's help, irrigation ditches were dug and crops were planted in the fertile valley. But with more people streaming into the valley looking for prime land, the Native Americans were moved to the San Carlos Reservation in 1877. Nearly 100 of them died during the brutal 180-mile march. Soon afterward, the land of the Rio Verde was opened to settlers.

Events

The fort holds special events throughout the year. In February, the Buffalo Soldiers that served at Fort Verde in the late 1880s are honored. Reenactors portray the all-black regiments in drills, riding demonstrations, and living-history presentations.

Fort Verde Days takes place the second weekend in October and features flag-raising and flag-lowering ceremonies, cavalry drills, living-history demonstrations, a fashion show, a vintage baseball game, and additional activities through the town.

A Victorian Christmas takes place through December with the fort adorned in beautiful period decorations. Candlelight tours are offered on select weekends.

AROUND TOWN

Camp Verde's annual Cornfest takes place in July with music, food, games, contests, kids' activities, and of course plenty of delicious sweet corn to munch. There's usually a vintage baseball game going at the parade ground of Fort Verde.

Picnic Areas

Eight picnic tables are spread across the grounds near the buildings.

Nearby Attractions

Montezuma Castle is an imposing five-story cliff dwelling that has been called the best-preserved example of Native American architecture in the Southwest. Built by the Sinagua people over 800 years ago, it perches high above the Beaver Creek floodplain. A deep alcove in the limestone wall provides protection from the elements and is no doubt responsible for the excellent condition of the ancient high-rise. The first Euro-American explorers to discover the structure presumed it to be Aztec in origin, hence the name. It was abandoned a century before the Aztec emperor Montezuma was born. 928-567-3322, www.nps.gov/moca.

A few miles away from Montezuma Castle is a related but very different experience. Montezuma Well is a detached unit of the national monument. But here the focus is on the natural limestone sinkhole that pumps out 1.5 million gallons of water each day from an underground spring. Several small cliff dwellings perch along the rocky rim of the well and the remnants of a prehistoric canal can still be seen. 11 miles separate the two park units. 928-567-3322, www.nps.gov/moca.

Verde Valley Archaeology Center is a small museum in downtown Camp Verde with exhibits on Sinagua culture, including rock art and pottery. As the official non-profit partner of Montezuma Castle and Tuzigoot national monuments, the center works to preserve the numerous heritage sites in the area. Ancient pit houses are found along an educational walking path. The center offers several programs through the year. 385 South Main Street, 928-567-0066, www.verdevalleyarchaeology.org.

Homolovi State Park

Nearest Town: Winslow.

Why Go: Discover Hopi ancestral villages on expansive grasslands above the Little Colorado River, as well as remnants of an old Mormon settlement.

Somehow it's what you don't see at Homolovi that touches you.

There are powerful forces at work amid these windswept grasslands, a connection to something positively ancient. A spirit surrounds this lonely place on the high plains near Winslow. As I walked these trails it occurred to me that somehow the silence is louder here. The spaces are wider and the sky feels bigger. The horizons are swept back beyond the horizon. I could see forever.

Homolovi is Hopi for "place of the little hills." The park protects Hopi ancestral villages. Four major pueblos exist within the park but only two are open to the public.

Additionally, there are pit houses and scattered artifacts. The sites date from three main periods: AD 620–850, AD 1050–1225, and AD 1260–1400.

They came for the water, of course.

Lifeblood of the Plains

The Little Colorado River winds along the western edge of the park. It doesn't look like much at first, a languid stream with a chocolaty flow. But don't be fooled. The wide greenbelt that traces the meandering channel attests to the river's volatile nature. It was this fertile floodplain that drew people to an otherwise inhospitable area.

The area appears to have been continuously occupied by the Ancestral Puebloans, sometime after 6000 BC. They were originally hunters and gatherers living in temporary camps and leaving little impact on the land. By the first century AD, they began cultivating crops like corn, squash, beans, and cotton. As they became more reliant on agriculture, they began developing more

The Hopi people still consider Homolovi to be part of their homeland. Courtesy of Arizona State Parks and Trails, Phoenix.

permanent dwellings, simple pit houses at first and later stone and masonry structures.

Of the four pueblos located within the park, the first were occupied between 1250 and 1300. The largest of these is Homolovi II, where 750 to 1,000 people resided. This 1,200-room pueblo was built during the fourteenth century by Hopis who traveled from their mesa-top villages during a time of drought to the hills above the Little Colorado.

Once the drought ended, frequent floods by the river prompted the remaining pueblos to be abandoned. Prior to 1400, the Homolovi residents made their way north to the Hopi villages. Their descendants return periodically to gather wild resources and visit shrines.

Living Villages

When the park opened, it was originally named Homolovi Ruins State Park. The Hopi tribe lobbied to drop the word "ruins" because they consider the ancient pueblos spiritually alive. In 2011 the parks board complied.

Don't come expecting clearly defined structures. The centuries have gnawed at them. But the work of unscrupulous pot-hunters proved far more destructive than time. By the 1960s a backhoe was being used to dig up the sites. The state park was established to prevent this continued devastation.

Yet the outlines of the villages are clearly visible and signage helps put everything in focus. In places, the park service has reconstructed walls or excavated a kiva.

The Homolovi Visitor Center includes a small museum with exhibits and artwork on display. Photo by the author.

Potsherds are scattered around, although most are small. Yet you don't have to search hard to find them. Visitors have placed some pieces atop stones for better viewing. While it is strictly forbidden to remove potsherds or any artifact, it's okay to touch.

I moved slowly through Homolovi I and II, reading signs that try to condense such an epic timeline into a few sentences. I scanned for artifacts but always my eyes strayed to distant horizons. Standing on the sun-splashed hills, I could see the outline of the San Francisco Peaks rising in the west. Hopis believe these mountains are the home of kachina spirits. Kachinas are supernatural beings with the power to bring the rain and other blessings.

Ultimately it's the landscape—quiet and vast—that tells much of the story. I tried to imagine this place with 1,000 souls living, working, and playing here. Suddenly the silence felt different. When I gazed north, I could see the three mesas, home of the Hopi villages. And I knew that this ancient story would continue.

Mormons Arrive

There's also a sort of secret chapter of Homolovi history. In addition to the Hopi lands and artifacts, the park contains a small cemetery, which is all that's left of the town of Sunset, an early Mormon community.

Brigham Young of the Church of Jesus Christ of Latter-day Saints appointed Lot Smith, a Mormon Battalion veteran, to lead an expedition to occupy the Little Colorado River Valley in 1876. It took six weeks for the 115 families to arrive at Sunset Crossing in the Arizona Territory and form settlements.

It proved to be a hard life, not uncommon to the frontier in those days. Attempts to dam the river failed, and frequent floods destroyed crops. Communities had to be relocated to higher ground and in between floods came the devastating droughts. The pioneers were relieved of their calling in 1881 with many going on to establish other missions. According to the handout available at the visitor center, Lot Smith was the last to leave in 1888.

All that remains of Sunset is a lonely graveyard atop a hill above the Little Colorado. The trail to Sunset Cemetery begins at the visitor center and follows an old road for 0.4 miles. It's a tidy fenced plot with a mix of historic and newer gravestones. Three of Lot Smith's children are buried here, one who died of scarlet fever, one who drowned in the river, and another who tragically died as a result of falling into a vat of boiling lye during soapmaking. Perhaps that's why Smith stayed the longest. He was loath to leave so much behind.

When You Go

Homolovi State Park is located near Winslow. Take Interstate 40 to Exit 257 and travel north 1.5 miles on Arizona 87. All day-use areas of the park are open from 8:00 a.m. to 5:00 p.m. 928-289-4106, azstateparks.com.

Fast Fact: Of the four Little Colorado River colonies settled by Mormons in 1876 (Sunset, Joseph City, Brigham City, and Obed), only Joseph City remains, 22 miles east of Winslow.

Admission

$ per vehicle (up to four adults).

Camping

The campground sits on the slope above the Little Colorado River and contains 52 sites. All but 9 have electric and 7 are ADA accessible. Every site has a picnic table and fire pit. There are no size restrictions on RVs.

Events

Guided tours of Homolovi IV are offered most weekends fall through spring. This is the oldest of the Homolovi pueblos and is generally closed to the public. Attendees will caravan in their own vehicles the 12 miles to Homolovi IV.

Suvoyuki Day gives visitors a chance to gain insight into the history and lifestyle of the Hopi people. Husked corn, cooked overnight in a roasting pit, is served to begin the day. Guided tours of the sites are offered. A Hopi marketplace features jewelry, baskets, pottery, and other wares made by local artists. The Hopis also share some of their traditional dances, which are rarely seen by the public. Suvoyuki Day takes place in August.

Petroglyph tours, pottery talks, star parties, and other similar events take place throughout the year. The star parties are especially popular. In 2018 the Winslow Homolovi Observatory opened, a great addition for an area far from city lights. The facility was a joint effort of the City of Winslow, the Hopi Tribe, the Little Colorado River Astronomy Club, and Arizona State Parks and Trails. It's open anytime, with a donated 14-inch telescope set up inside. Homolovi is the first Arizona state park to feature an observatory.

Picnic Areas

Picnic tables with shade are located at the visitor center, along the road to Homolovi II and at the site of Homolovi II.

Trails

The park includes a handful of short, easy trails.

Nusungvö ("Place of Rest" in Hopi) is a 1.2-mile trail connecting the visitor center to the campground.

Tsu'vö ("Path of the Rattlesnake" in Hopi) squeezes through twin buttes crowned with boulder slabs, the most distinctive features amid the rolling grasslands. The 0.5-mile loop passes faint petroglyphs and milling-stone areas.

Diné makes a 1.5-mile gentle climb to Diné Point atop a knoll, and connects with the other two trails.

Sunset Cemetery can be accessed by a 0.4-mile walk down an old road.

Homolovi I, located near the river, is reached by a short stroll from the parking area and through the site.

Homolovi II features a 0.5-mile paved path that's wheelchair accessible and lined with informational signage.

Visitor Center

The visitor center includes exhibits and artifacts of the park sites and Hopi culture. There's also a memorial to the 10 Hopi code talkers of World War II. While the service of the Navajo code talkers has become well known in recent years, other tribes also used their language to create a secret code that was never broken by the enemy. Hopi code talkers served in the Pacific campaign assisting the US Military Intelligence Service in the Marshall Islands, New Caledonia, and the Philippines during the war.

Nearby Attractions

Encompassing 5,000 acres in northern Arizona, Rock Art Ranch is a working cattle ranch located between Winslow and Holbrook and is also home to one of the best-preserved and most extensive collections of ancient petroglyphs in the world. Tucked away in scenic Chevelon Canyon, panels of images etched into the rocks adorn cliff faces, alcoves, and overhangs. Rock Art Ranch features a museum stocked with artifacts found on the property, a Navajo hogan and sweathouse, and ancient pueblos. Reservations are required for a visit. Directions will be given at that time. 928-386-5047.

After gazing across the tawny plains of Homolovi, you may yearn for a jolt of color. You'll find a lavish display at nearby Little Painted Desert County Park, a spectacular overlook above a sea of rolling multihued badlands. Despite the name, it hasn't been maintained as a park for years. From the high perch, you gaze down at vivid formations, seamed with color and gnawed by erosion. There are a few shaded picnic tables and a short, rough road that travels along the rim, offering a few different vantage points, all of them beautiful. Little Painted Desert is located about 12 miles north of Homolovi on Arizona 87, on the west side of the highway.

While the most famous corner on all of Route 66 can be found in Winslow, Remembrance Garden is not so well known. But it should be. Remembrance Garden was constructed using two beams from the wreckage of the World Trade Center. The two rusted steel girders—one 14 feet high and the other 15 feet high—are anchored in concrete, rising side by side as homage to the Twin Towers. These are said to be the largest pieces of debris from the World Trade Center that were shipped to any town. Flanked by an American flag and marked by a single plaque, the roadside

Jerome State Historic Park tells the story of a mountainside mining camp. Photo by the author.

memorial is a quiet, reflective spot on the eastern edge of Winslow.

Jerome State Historic Park

Nearest Town: Jerome.

Why Go: A visit to picturesque Jerome is one of Arizona's best day trips and should begin with a tour of the Douglas Mansion, now converted to a sprawling museum that explains the rowdy and lucrative mining history of the town.

Jerome has never paid much heed to calendars. It didn't right from the start.

By the turn of the twentieth century, the Wild West was winding down across Arizona. Geronimo was living as a prisoner of war at Fort Sill, Oklahoma; it had been almost two decades since shots rang out at the O.K. Corral; and continued expansion of the railroad was a civilizing influence. Most towns on the former frontier were settling down, but not Jerome.

The mile-high boomtown was still running wide open, a rowdy mix of saloons, brothels, and violence in the streets. In 1903 the *New York Sun* called Jerome "the wickedest town in the West." And they hadn't even hit their heyday yet.

Boomtown

The first mining claims in the area were filed in 1876 on Mingus Mountain, west of the present-day town. The early prospectors sold out to a group that formed the United Verde Copper Company in 1883. Their principal backer was New York financier Eugene Jerome, and the ramshackle camp built atop Cleopatra Hill was named in his honor.

While the mine was obviously a good producer, the high cost of transporting ore from such a remote location outstripped profits. When wealthy mining magnate William A. Clark took over the company,

Fast Fact: Eugene Jerome never visited his namesake town. Jerome was a cousin of Jennie Jerome, mother of Winston Churchill.

he used his fortune to build a narrow-gauge railroad, thus reducing freighting costs. Once it was completed in 1894, the United Verde became the largest producing copper mine in the Arizona Territory.

In 1912 James S. Douglas, known as Rawhide Jimmy, began development of the Little Daisy Mine. Two years later, he hit a bonanza when he discovered a second ore body. The Little Daisy would eventually produce $125 million in ore.

The House on a Hill

While he was rolling in dough, Rawhide Jimmy decided to throw up some swanky digs. He built the Douglas Mansion on a hill just above his mine. Constructed of adobe bricks made on-site, the rambling 8,700-square-foot structure was loaded with amenities. It featured a wine cellar, a billiard room, marble showers, steam heat, and a very modernistic central vacuum system. The opulent home also served as lodging for traveling mining officials and investors.

Yet nothing lasts forever. Copper production peaked in 1929 but the Great Depression took a toll and the seemingly endless veins of ore eventually began to peter out. The Little Daisy shut down in 1938. Phelps Dodge had taken over the United Verde Mine three years earlier, and they kept it limping long until 1953, when it was shuttered at last. Jerome's mining days were no more.

It was an incredible run. Although gold, silver, and other metals were mined in Jerome, copper was king. The ores produced by Jerome mines totaled more than $1 billion. They were among the richest copper deposits ever found in the world.

Jerome experienced the typical boom-bust cycle of mining towns, except in a bigger and harder way than most. Blasting in the mines took a toll as buildings collapsed and others slid down the hill. In the 1920s,

Examples of minerals pulled from Jerome mines are on display inside the Douglas Mansion. Photo by the author.

15,000 residents lived here. By the time the last mine closed in 1953, fewer than 50 remained, earning Jerome status as Arizona's largest ghost town. A handful of folks that stayed behind formed a historical society and began patching the scars and knitting the bones of this tumbledown town.

Come for the View

Rawhide Jimmy moved to Canada in 1939 and died a decade later. His sons put the vacant mansion up for sale but with no success. In 1962 they donated it to the state. Remodeling and restoration began, and museum exhibits were installed. It opened as a state park in 1965.

The park preserves the Douglas Mansion—perched on a hill, apart from town—and the surrounding two acres. Not many museums have such a spectacular setting. Views spill across the Verde Valley to the red rocks of Sedona and the distinctive profile of the San Francisco Peaks.

The house museum tells the story of the Jerome area, mining, and the Douglas family. When you enter the home, the large living room serves as the welcome center and gift shop. Other rooms are filled with artifacts, historic photographs, minerals, and memorabilia. A 30-minute video presentation plays throughout the day.

They have a 3-D model of the mountainous burg that shows not just the hills but the 88 miles of tunnels dug out beneath them—beneath the very ground where you're standing. If you already feel that Jerome seems rather precarious clinging to such steep slopes, the model will do nothing to ease your fears.

The exhibits continue outside. Peek in the carriage house to see the big buggy that Rawhide Jimmy drove around northern Arizona. It gained a measure of fame when it appeared in the movie *Oklahoma*.

Surrounding the manse are pieces of mining equipment, including the one that intrigues me the most.

That Ain't Honey

Whenever my job starts feeling stressful, I think of the guy who had to handle the honey wagon in the mines.

As charming as it sounds, the honey wagon was actually a rolling toilet used by miners deep underground. Any kind of hard-rock mining had to be grueling work, toiling away hundreds of feet below ground in cramped, dimly lit tunnels. And one guy had to be in charge of the wheeled, boxy two-seat commode.

He would hand responsibility over to someone else when his shift ended, because mines operated 24 hours a day. Then he would head for the surface, maybe throw back a few whiskies in one of Jerome's many saloons before retiring to his shack for some shut-eye. Likely he lay there a while each night staring at the ceiling and wondering how he ended up here, if maybe he should try his luck at the next boomtown, and praying that the jerk on the other

shift emptied the honey wagon instead of leaving it for him. Then after a few hours he would crawl out of his cot and go do it all over again.

When stacked against the duties of the honey-wagon operator, my job seems remarkably stress-free.

A Ghost Town Reborn

Along with a new state park, Jerome experienced a counterculture renaissance beginning in the 1960s, a polite way of saying hippies moved in. They snapped up real estate on the cheap and opened shops, restaurants, and art galleries. Most importantly, they injected Jerome with the relaxed, carefree vibe still prevalent today.

If a chunk of the '60s is kept alive in this mountainside oasis, it should come as no surprise. The calendar doesn't mean much in Jerome. Never has. Everything moves at a different pace. The town's 450 residents are proud to claim that Jerome exists on Mountain Stranded Time.

Historic buildings have been restored and house an eclectic assortment of shops, galleries, eateries, and wine bars that line

Managing the honey wagon was probably not a highly sought after job in the mines. Photo by the author.

the twisted, narrow streets. But don't worry, there are still a couple of classic saloons thumping with live music on weekends, a nice homage to a rowdy past.

When You Go

Jerome State Historic Park is located at 100 Douglas Road. It is open from 8:30 a.m. to 5:00 p.m. 928-634-5381, azstateparks.com.

Admission

Adults and youths (7–13), $. Free admission for children 6 and under.

Events

AROUND TOWN

The Jerome Art Walk takes place the first Saturday of each month from 5:00 to 8:00 p.m. with galleries and shops staying open late. Many venues host receptions with food, drink, live music, and artist demonstrations.

A legacy of violent deaths—both in the mines and in the streets—has led to a healthy population of restless, lingering spirits. So it's no surprise that Halloween has become Jerome's Mardi Gras. The annual Ghost Walk takes place every October, featuring dramatic presentations of how some notable characters met their demise.

The biggest event of the season is the Volunteer Fire Department Halloween Dance, a tradition since 1974. It began as a fundraiser for the local fire department and continues to grow. Other towns celebrate Halloween but Jerome marinates in the joyous indulgence of it. The dance takes place

at the community center known simply as Spook Hall but tends to spread through the streets. Prizes are given for best costumes but bring your A game. You'll be up against some serious competition.

Picnic Areas

A shady picnic area with tables and lovely views is located on the property.

Nearby Attractions

After seeing where the Douglas family lived, take a look at their business. Adjacent to the state park is the Audrey Shaft Headframe Park. The Audrey Headframe, completed in 1918, is the largest wooden headframe still standing in Arizona. It was utilized in extracting $125 million worth of ore from the Little Daisy Mine. Visitors can stand on a glass platform above a 1,900-foot shaft. That's 650 feet taller than the Empire State Building. Operated by the Jerome Historical Society, the park displays other pieces of mining equipment including a man-cage used to raise and lower miners through the depths.

The state park is full of rich details of the mining history of Jerome. But of course not everyone lived in a mansion in those days. The Mine Museum gives you a taste of life for everyday residents. Artifacts include gambling paraphernalia, saloon equipment, household goods, hospital equipment, and exhibits on the role played by the Chinese and other ethnicities. There's also a Colt pistol used by Marshal Johnny Hudgens who gunned down more than one ne'er-do-well in the streets of Jerome. 200 Main Street, 928-634-5477, jeromehistorical society.com.

When you visit a ghost town, it's only natural to look for ghosts. A couple of local tour companies can help you play Scooby-Doo. They'll even set you up with electro-magnetic field (EMF) readers to measure paranormal activity. Tours of Jerome and

Ghost Town Tours each offer a variety of outings of different lengths. You can choose tours focused on the gritty history of the region or pursue residents of the spirit world. Custom tours are also available. Tours of Jerome: 928-639-4361, www.tour sofjerome.com; Ghost Town Tours: 928-634-6118, ghosttowntours.org.

Lyman Lake State Park

Nearest Town: Springerville.
Why Go: Boaters seeking open water will appreciate this 1,500-acre reservoir, while landlubbers will enjoy the hiking trails, ancient rock art, and comfortable cabins.

I had never had an entire state park to myself before, but Lyman Lake was all mine.

The sprawling 1,500-acre reservoir spreads across the high plains of northeastern Arizona. At an elevation of 6,000 feet,

Lyman is fed by the snowmelt from the slopes of Mount Baldy and Escudilla Mountain, the second and third highest mountains in the state. And it all belonged to me since I was the only one there. All I needed was a flag to plant to claim it as my own.

Stormy Weather

Driving north from Springerville to Lyman Lake State Park, I watched a massive monsoon storm roll across the grasslands. It was a wall of scowling dark sky, a veil of midnight falling in late afternoon. But I kept going because big shafts of sunshine rode on the heels of the fast-moving storm and looked very inviting.

My timing was perfect. I arrived at the same time the blue sky did in that quiet post-storm calm. But evidence of the downpour was widespread. Water dripped from every surface. Washes and arroyos were torrents. The parking lot was a pond,

Lyman Lake sits on the high plains north of Springerville. Photo by the author.

A stormy summer sunset streaks across Lyman Lake. Photo by the author.

the beach was submerged, and kids would need a snorkel to romp in the playground sandbox.

It was a hushed and beautiful scene but eerie because no one else was around. There was no ranger at the entry gate, just a sign saying to proceed to the store. But since it was after 4:30 p.m., the store was closed. I rambled around the park for 15 minutes, enjoying the fresh-scrubbed air before discovering I wasn't the last man on Earth.

I finally spotted a couple of others emerging from the campground. They moved tentatively, no doubt a little shaky if they had ridden out such a ferocious storm in a tent or thin-skinned RV. They seemed surprised to see me, and we gazed across the distance for a few moments, finally exchanging waves just to verify that we were not in fact shambling walkers in some kind of zombie apocalypse.

Big Water

Lyman Lake was created as an irrigation reservoir by damming the Little Colorado River. It is by far the largest lake in the region. With 1,500 acres, Lyman is one of the few bodies of water in the White Mountains with no size restrictions on boats. If you've got an aircraft carrier just taking up space in your driveway, load it on the trailer and head for the high country.

Lyman features a few twisting channels, some secluded coves, and a big expanse of open water. Visitors can have any type of experience on the water they want. Portions of the west end of Lyman are buoyed off and restricted as a no-wake zone, so anglers aren't disturbed by an armada of speedboats and water skiers. With miles of curving shoreline to explore, Lyman is a paradise for kayakers. Swimmers have their own quiet beach, at least when it's not temporarily underwater. The beach is located behind the park store, and boats and fishing are not allowed.

For landlubbers like me, a few hiking trails wind through the park. Since they were likely submerged at the time of my visit, I prowled the shoreline, gazing at the wild, monsoony sky. I hung around long enough to catch a sweet sunset and then made plans to return.

Hiking and History

I visited Lyman Lake two days later on a Saturday morning with plenty of sunshine mingled with billowy white clouds. First thing I wondered was who were all these people and what were they doing in my park. Although I hadn't officially invoked squatter's rights, I still felt some proprietary ownership. Oh well. It was a beautiful morning and the park is big enough so I magnanimously decided to let everyone stay.

To be honest, it wasn't that much of a crowd. Despite its immense size, Lyman Lake is still very much a hidden gem. The White Mountains sparkle with dozens of lakes, so this big pond sitting just outside the forests gets overlooked. That's a shame.

I checked in at the store, which serves as the visitor center, and got directions to Rattlesnake Ruins. For centuries, ancestors of the Hopi, Zuni, and other Pueblo clans

Fast Fact: Film legend John Wayne once owned a ranch in Eagar and was a frequent and beloved visitor in the community.

lived in the region, planting crops along the fertile floodplain of the river. One partially excavated village sits toward the eastern end of the lake.

Rattlesnake Point Ruins are located about a mile and a half down an unpaved road that was a little chewed by the storm but still manageable. I arrived to find the gate locked, which the ranger at the store said might be the case. With her advance permission, I climbed over.

There are three rooms, sheltered by a roof from the elements, with interpretive signage. The outline of another pueblo is nearby. These and other villages through the area date back to AD 1300–1400.

Other evidence of these ancient tribes can be found in displays of petroglyphs, and I went to check them out next. The short Peninsula Petroglyph Trail climbs among the jumbled boulders on a little jut of land near the beach. The quarter-mile trail clambers up some steps leading to a few carvings. Several additional pathways loop around the rock-strewn hill and offer nice lake views.

Hilltop Vistas

The Pointe Trail is the cream of the bunch. It's just a mile loop atop a small mesa at water's edge but makes a wonderful high perch to enjoy stunning and ever-changing panoramas. I love this little jaunt. After making a moderate climb, the pathway circles the hill, so I got to witness all facets of Lyman Lake. Or most of them. This big reservoir stretches through the valley for such a long way that I still couldn't see the end of it.

I was content to study the details visible

at every bend of the trail. A smoochy couple of anglers had to break off midhug because she got a bite. A pontoon boat launched from the boat ramp and virtually disappeared in a matter of seconds, becoming just a speck in the vast expanse of open water. A speedboat roared across the lake, bouncing in the chop. A water skier glided through a long channel. I spotted another boat towing something too round to be a single skier, but it wasn't until it passed below me that I could see it was some kind of toboggan carrying a couple of kids. Their shrieks of joy came wafting up out of the canyon.

It was the kind of moment that made me glad I hadn't chased everyone out.

When You Go

Lyman Lake State Park is 17 miles north of Springerville, on US 180/191. 928-337-4441, azstateparks.com.

Admission

$ per vehicle (up to four adults).

Boating

Lyman Lake has no size restrictions on boats, motors, or personal watercraft. Water skiers should use the center of the lake and the northwest end. There are two boat ramps in the park.

Cabins

Lyman features eight heated and air-conditioned cabins, each with a full-sized bed, one or two sets of bunk beds, a table, chairs, and a covered wooden porch. Bring your own bedding or sleeping bags, towels, utensils, and so on. And pack a flashlight for nighttime walks to the restrooms and showers.

Camping

There are 56 campsites available in the park, 38 with electric and water hookups.

Lyman Lake provides recreational opportunities for all ages. Courtesy of Arizona State Parks and Trails, Phoenix.

Fishing

Anglers can catch largemouth bass, catfish, carp, and walleye. Fishing licenses are available at the store. A valid Arizona fishing license is required for anglers 10 years and older.

Picnic Areas

There are picnic tables with shaded ramadas at the day-use area and near the Peninsula Petroglyph Trailhead.

Swimming

Lyman Lake has a designated swimming area between the park store and the peninsula. Swimming is not allowed outside the designated area. In all situations, swimmers should exercise caution. There is no lifeguard on duty, so swimming is at your own risk.

Trails

The 2-mile Buffalo Trail cuts through the interior of the park and involves some steep inclines and steps. It's named for a herd of bison that were once kept near the park entrance.

Peninsula Petroglyph Trail makes a quarter-mile climb up a boulder-strewn hill with a few prehistoric symbols etched into the rocks. Additional pathways clamber up and over the hill, adding an extra 1.5 miles of hiking and affording a variety of lake views.

The Pointe Trail starts from the picnic area across from the store and climbs some steps up a moderate incline. Once you're atop the hill, you'll enjoy the best views in the park. A 1-mile loop circles the crest, which has a couple of benches and plenty of good sitting rocks positioned for maximum panorama-ogling possibilities. Even with shady tables below, this is the primo picnic spot in the park. The trail can also be accessed from the group-use area.

Visitor Center / Store

A small market serves as visitor center and sells food, drinks, bait, and supplies.

Nearby Attractions

With multiple museums and exhibits housed in one building, Springerville Heritage Center should be your first stop when you hit town. The historic schoolhouse has been restored and includes a gallery of work from local artists. A plush little theatre shows a video documenting the region, and there's a multimedia volcanic exhibit. The Casa Malpais Museum includes exhibits on some of the early inhabitants (928-333-5375, www.casamalpais.org), and the Renee Cushman Museum features a collection of paintings, tapestries, and china, including an engraving by Rembrandt. 418 East Main Street, 928-333-2656, ext. 230.

You can practically follow your nose to the Red Rock Ranch and Farms. Located in Concho, this spread is likely the most fragrant agricultural plot in all Arizona, with fields of luscious lavender. The idea was to grow organic vegetables, but Michael and Christine Teeple soon realized that the lavender they grew for landscaping purposes was absolutely thriving. Now with 35,000 plants, Red Rock produces some of the

> **Fast Fact**: Casa Malpais is the premier archaeological site in the White Mountains. It was built about AD 1250 and features a solar calendar, a great kiva, and rock art. Guided tours of the site originate at the museum.

finest lavender in the world. The farm hosts a Lavender Festival at the end of June that includes lavender-growing talks, cooking lessons and tastings, demonstrations, refreshments, and music. Vineyards have been added to the flowery fields, and regular wine-tasting events have been added to the schedule. www.redrockfarms.com.

The Apache County Historical Society Museum in St. Johns may be small, but it's full of surprises, including intact tusks of a wooly mammoth. Exhibits cover the diverse populations of Apache County, including numerous Native American tribes and Hispanic and Mormon settlers. Mixed in with arrowheads, weapons, tools, musical instruments, clothing, and diaries is a petrified snail as big as a dinner plate. How often do you stumble across one of those? Outdoor exhibits include pioneer cabins, wagons, and spooky steel jail cells. Run by volunteers, museum hours are limited. 180 West Cleveland Street, 928-337-4737.

Red Rock State Park

Nearest Town: Sedona.

Why Go: With 5 miles of interconnected trails spreading across the hills above Oak Creek and a visitor center brimming with environmental exhibits, this park offers a great introduction to the unique red rock landscape of Sedona.

It's just a house on a hill. But what a hill, and what a house. It's a dream home that serves as a stark reminder that not every dream comes true.

The House of Apache Fires sits on a hilltop in Red Rock State Park.
Photo by the author.

The House of Apache Fires perches atop a bluff in the middle of Red Rock State Park. The pueblo-style structure has 360-degree views of sandstone cliffs, grassy meadows, and a shade-draped creek.

Newlyweds Jack and Helen Frye fell in love with Sedona's beauty in the early 1940s while flying overhead. He was an aviation pioneer and the president of TWA, and she had studied and practiced as an artist. They began acquiring property, which would become a 700-acre spread known as Smoke Trail Ranch. Construction of their new home began in 1947.

Designed by Helen, who envisioned a Hopi pueblo, the house proved to be a massive undertaking. Exterior walls were made of flat red Sedona rocks and interiors featured ceilings of exposed beams overlaid with layers of smaller poles. Nearly every

Fast Fact: Jack Frye was a true visionary. His work led to the development of the first pressurized modern airliner, designed to fly at higher altitudes above the weather. As a pilot he established numerous speed records. He was inducted into the National Aviation Hall of Fame.

room was built on a different level and offered panoramic views.

Sadly, the couple never got to truly enjoy the fruits of their labor. The Fryes divorced in 1950 before the house was completed. I often wonder if the house broke up the marriage. Probably not. There were likely other issues involved. Still, the Fryes wouldn't be the first couple that couldn't handle the stress of a home-improvement project.

Lessons Learned

If all classrooms were as intriguing as Red Rock State Park, I wouldn't have slept through most of my senior year in high school. The park is a 286-acre nature preserve and environmental- education center that comes wrapped in gorgeous scenery.

Just try to visit Red Rock without learning something, I dare you. It's virtually impossible. The visitor center brims with informative, hands-on exhibits covering geology, archaeology, wildlife, and plant life. The theater plays a short film on Sedona and the surrounding area. And guided hikes are a daily event. Red Rock is the nerd of the state park system.

I use the guided hikes at Red Rock as a refresher course. While I'm reasonably knowledgeable about local plant life, spring always throws a few curves. Every spring a new batch of wildflowers emerges. I know plenty of them but always want to learn more. So I'll tag along on a naturalist-led hike at Red Rock and let their expert identify them all. By the end of the walk, I'll fairly ooze knowledge.

Unfortunately, many flowering plants have short life spans. Out of sight, out of mind. By the next year I will need another tutorial. This just means that I will be forced once again to go hiking into flower-dotted red rock hills on a balmy spring day. Tough break.

Creek Walks and Hill Climbs

A 5-mile network of interconnected trails loops through the park. The Kisva Trail and Smoke Trail make easy strolls along the banks of Oak Creek beneath the shade of cottonwoods, sycamores, velvet ashes, and alder trees. The perennial stream is the centerpiece of the park, a liquid dagger that carves a riparian corridor from arid uplands. Three bridge crossings span the water. Swimming or wading in the creek is not permitted.

Other trails scramble into the rolling hills, but none of the routes proves strenuous. The Eagle's Nest Trail reaches the highest point in the park and it's only a 300-foot climb. You'll enjoy views of distant formations like Cathedral Rock and Seven Warriors from several vantage points. You can also exit the park on foot via the east gate to connect to other Forest Service trails.

While most trails in the park are off-limits to bicycles, outside trails can be accessed. A common route taken by bikers is the 6.2-mile Cathedral Bike Loop, which leads out of the park through the east gate, down Verde Valley School Road, across Oak Creek (no bridge), and back to the park's entrance on the Upper Red Rock Loop Road.

The Lime Kiln Trail, which connects Dead Horse Ranch State Park with Red Rock State Park, is another popular bike ride. It's located just outside the entrance gate. The Lime Kiln is 15 miles long and follows a historic wagon road.

The House of Apache Fires can be seen from several points in the park. The closest access is provided by the Apache Fire Trail. However, the building is not currently open to visitors.

Oak Creek creates a riparian habitat through the heart of Red Rock State Park. Photo by the author.

After her divorce, Helen Frye took ownership of the ranch. She lived in the unfinished house for a number of years. Attempts were made to complete the project, first as an art center in the 1950s, then as a resort in the 1970s, and finally as a spiritual retreat when Helen became enamored of a religious group called Eckankar. Helen died in 1979.

The house and remaining acreage were purchased by the state of Arizona in the late 1980s, and Red Rock opened in 1991. The house was already in a state of disrepair, having sustained serious damage through the decades. A 1967 snowstorm collapsed part of the roof. A windstorm in the 1990s exacerbated the issue. Elegant as it appears from the outside, the House of Apache Fires teeters on the verge of collapse. The Benefactors of Red Rock State Park have raised funds and begun work to stabilize and restore the home to a glory it never quite achieved.

When You Go

Red Rock State Park is located 3 miles southwest of Sedona. It is open from 8:00 a.m. to 5:00 p.m. year-round, with extended hours Friday to Sunday, from the second weekend in May through the end of August, when it stays open till dusk. Last entry is a half hour before the park closes. 4050 Red Rock Loop Road, 928-282-6907, azstateparks.com.

Swimming is prohibited at Red Rock State Park but is available at nearby Red Rock Crossing. Courtesy of Mike Koopsen, Sedona.

Admission

Adults and youths (7–13), $. Free admission for children 6 and under. Pets are not allowed at this park.

Events

Daily naturalist hikes leave from the visitor center each morning. Knowledgeable volunteers discuss subjects such as geology, wildlife, history, archaeology, and plant life on these guided hikes. No reservations needed. Hikes start at 10:00 a.m. September to May, and at 9:00 a.m. June to August.

Bird walks take place every Wednesday and Saturday throughout the year. Times vary with the seasons: 7:00 a.m. June to August; 8:00 a.m. March to May, and also September to November; and 9:00 a.m. December to February.

Full-moon hikes provide visitors with an amazing show. First, you hike out to witness the setting sun that only deepens the rich colors of the rocky pinnacles. Then you've got a front-row seat to watch the moon rise, full and fat and impossibly large. Then enjoy an easy hike back to the visitor center in the shimmering light. Each full-moon hike is led by a knowledgeable park ranger and covers 2 miles. Reservations are required at least 24 hours before the hike. There's a small fee in addition to the park admission.

AROUND TOWN

Held every February, the Sedona International Film Festival is a celebration of some of the best independent films from around the world. The festival screens more than 160 movies over nine days and attracts a roster of screenwriters, directors, and actors who participate in eagerly anticipated workshops.

The Sedona Plein Air Festival unleashes two dozen master painters on the amazing landscape every October. Watch as they instantly commit the essence and details of a variety of locations to the canvas. The weeklong festival celebrates the creativity that Sedona always seems to inspire and includes receptions, exhibitions, workshops, and lectures.

Picnic Areas

There are picnic tables near the visitor center, in addition to the Hummingbird Patio, and some larger group sites.

Trails

The Red Rock trail system is well maintained with good signage. Many junctions include signs with maps or directional arrows. But since there are numerous trails in close proximity, it's always a good idea to carry the handy trail map available at the entry gate or visitor center. The Eagle's Nest Loop and Apache Fire Loop ramble into the hills and are connected by Coyote Ridge Trail. These three link to the Kisva Trail, which parallels Oak Creek and also provides access to the short loop of the Yavapai Ridge Trail.

Visitor Center

The Miller Visitor Center includes interpretive exhibits detailing the habitats found in the park, early human habitation, and wildlife. The movie theater shows a short film upon request, *The Natural Wonders of Sedona: Timeless Beauty*. It recounts Sedona's history and takes you on an aerial tour of the red rocks, which is appropriate since Jack and Helen Frye were first smitten with the landscape while flying overhead. There is outside seating at the Hummingbird Patio, a beautiful garden filled with flowers and a variety of bird feeders.

Nearby Attractions

After spending time gazing at the cool, clear water of Oak Creek, you may be sorely tempted to dip in a toe or a torso. You don't have to travel far from the park to get soaking wet. And you can do it at an iconic spot, Crescent Moon Picnic Site, known locally as Red Rock Crossing. The image of Oak Creek flowing in front of majestic Cathedral Rock is one of the most photographed spots in the Southwest. Don't be surprised to see radiant brides and glowing grooms posing for their wedding portrait on the rocky banks. Mosey upstream a ways and you'll find some sweet pools for wading, splashing, and swimming. There are picnic tables, restrooms, and drinking water available as well. This is a fee site. 928-203-2900, www.fs.usda.gov/coconino.

Sedona's most compelling work of art doesn't hang in a gallery. It rises from the ground and merges with surrounding towers of stone. The Chapel of the Holy Cross was designed by sculptor Marguerite Brunswig Staude and completed in 1957. The chapel perches above the valley floor, thrusting upward between two burly pillars of rock. The interior of the chapel is simple and unadorned. A few benches, some tapestries, and flickering candles create a serene, meditative oasis, while soft sunlight streams through the floor-to-ceiling window. 780 Chapel Road, 928-282-7545, www.chapeloftheholycross.com.

Nestled on the banks of Oak Creek in Sedona sits Tlaquepaque Arts and Crafts Village, a collection of Spanish-style buildings reminiscent of a Mexican hamlet. Cobblestone walkways meander past vine-covered walls and beneath stone archways. Graceful Arizona sycamores shade the courtyards where shoppers stroll past splashing fountains and beds bursting with flowers. Tlaquepaque houses a collection of galleries, shops, and restaurants. 336 Arizona 179, 928-282-4838, www.tlaq.com.

Riordan Mansion State Historic Park

Nearest Town: Flagstaff.

Why Go: Step back in time when you tour this 40-room mansion, one of the finest examples of American Arts and Crafts–style architecture open to the public, once owned by prominent Flagstaff pioneer families.

All that's missing is a big old hole in the ground. Then this place would be world famous.

Beginning in 1902, Charles Whittlesey was working out the details for a dramatic hotel to be perched on the very edge of the Grand Canyon. He wanted to use Oregon pine in the construction but had a question regarding the appetites of local Arizona insects. Whittlesey was chief architect for the Atchison, Topeka and Santa Fe Railway. The hotel he was designing at the canyon was to be the famed El Tovar.

Whittlesey took his insect query to the president of the largest lumber business in the area. Timothy Riordan ran the Arizona Lumber and Timber Company in Flagstaff. Once the talk turned away from hungry bugs, Riordan asked if the architect would be interested in designing homes for him and his younger brother, Michael.

Surprisingly, Whittlesey took on the little side project. The architect envisioned nearly identical twin homes for the brothers. There would be circular floor plans with seven bedrooms in the east wing, eight in the west wing. Each house included servant quarters, downstairs offices for the men, and stained-glass windows in the dining and breakfast rooms. They would be connected by a large common room.

Work began in November 1903. Of course, one of the advantages of operating a large lumber mill is having access to plenty of materials and men. A mere nine months later, before the El Tovar opened, the families were moving into the building that today is known as Riordan Mansion.

Fancy Digs

It's not everywhere that big, burly log cabins are labeled mansions, but that's just how we roll in Arizona. Don't be fooled by the rustic exterior of log-slab siding, hand-split wooden shingles, and volcanic stone arches. The sprawling homes definitely qualify as a mansion.

The homes combined for a total of 40 rooms and 13,000 square feet and featured

Snow blankets the grounds of Riordan Mansion in Flagstaff.
Courtesy of Arizona State Parks and Trails, Phoenix.

all-modern conveniences like central heat, hot and cold running water, and electric lights. The open floor plan, exposed structural elements, built-in features, and Gustav Stickley furniture reflected the Arts and Crafts style of architecture that was beginning to take hold in many parts of the country—although it was still a rarity in the Southwest.

The stuffy, fussy Victorian era was losing steam. The Arts and Crafts movement celebrated simplicity, craftsmanship, and natural beauty. More than anything else, the building provided the Riordans with a strong sense of place. With its use of ponderosa pine and native stone, the manse is rooted in the expansive northern Arizona forests. It looks like the El Tovar's country cousin, sitting atop a low hill in the Flagstaff pines.

Fast Fact: The El Tovar opened on the South Rim of the Grand Canyon in January 1905. It is the most renowned of all buildings designed by Charles Whittlesey.

Meet the Riordans

The Riordan brothers moved from the Midwest to Flagstaff in the 1880s. They worked first as managers of a lumber company, later purchasing it. Under their guidance, the Arizona Lumber and Timber Company turned into the area's largest employer.

By the time their new homes were completed, the Riordans were the very definition of pillars of the community. They were instrumental in building the first Catholic church in town, establishing the first library, building the school that would become Northern Arizona University, paving the way for Lowell Observatory, and even creating a brand-new county. Coconino County was carved from massive Yavapai County, and the growing burg of Flagstaff was chosen as the new county seat.

And then there's this curious fact: The brothers married sisters. Timothy married Caroline Metz, and Michael tied the knot with Elizabeth Metz. If it had happened just over a century later, the Riordans would have had their own reality show. Two brothers married to two sisters and living in a mansion together with an assortment of eight kids? That's a concept guaranteed to get the studio green light.

In August 1904 Timothy and Caroline, along with their two daughters, Mary and Anna, moved into the east wing of the big, rambling home. Michael and Elizabeth and their six children occupied the west wing. The two houses were connected in the center by a large common area known as "the cabin," which was used by both families for recreation and entertainment.

Preserving the Past

The property stayed in the Riordan family until it was donated to Arizona State Parks. The east wing of Riordan Mansion opened to the public in 1983. Blanche Riordan Chambers, daughter of Michael and Elizabeth, lived in the west wing until her death in 1985.

Guided tours of the log and stone

Fast Fact: In 1903 Timothy Riordan dammed a low-lying valley southeast of town to capture runoff from winter snowmelt. He named the reservoir for his first-born daughter. Lake Mary continues to be a significant water source and popular recreation area for Flagstaff.

---

manse are given daily at the top of the hour. Knowledgeable docents lead visitors through the east wing, which looks very much as it did in 1904. Rooms are packed with original artifacts, furnishings, and personal mementos. It feels so comfortable and lived-in, you almost expect the Riordan family to walk through the door mid-tour and politely ask what everyone is doing in their house.

The place is a treasure trove of period furniture, including 20 pieces by Gustav Stickley, a leader of the Arts and Crafts movement in America. All were purchased for the house when it was first constructed. Found among the collection are rare inlay furnishings by designer Harvey Ellis, some of the very few of his pieces not in private hands. Hardcore Stickley buffs will be thrilled to know that Riordan Mansion also contains four original pieces by Leopold and John George Stickley, younger brothers of Gustav.

Noting the pristine condition of these priceless furnishings, all I could think was that the Riordans raised extremely well-behaved children. Yet despite being surrounded by so many artistic treasures, I found my favorite part of the tour to be a simple but elegant porch swing suspended from the living-room ceiling. Who needs anything as mundane as a sofa? During the winter the swing faced the fireplace, but it could be turned during warmer months to face the outdoors.

What an utter stroke of genius. As a man who once bought a house because I fell in love with the porch, I salute the Riordans. All homes should feel this welcoming. That playful spirit is evident throughout the residence. Not to sound like a realtor but this is a very special property. This house that has been vacant for decades feels warm and homey. It connects us to the people who lived here in a wonderfully intimate way.

The tour concludes on the first floor of

Riordan Mansion is a treasure of Arts and Crafts–style architecture. Courtesy of Arizona State Parks and Trails, Phoenix.

the west wing, which has been laid out as an informal museum. Amid the furnishings and architectural details are displays about the family, the Arts and Crafts movement, and the history of Flagstaff.

All visitors that take the mansion tour are given an opportunity to explore the estate grounds. A handy brochure points out many of the significant details along the paved path.

When You Go

Riordan Mansion State Historic Park is located at 409 West Riordan Road. The park is open from 9:30 a.m. to 5:00 p.m. during the summer season (May 1–October 31). During winter (November 1–April 30), the hours are 10:30 a.m. to 5:00 p.m. Thursday through Monday. The park is closed Tuesday and Wednesday during winter. 928-779-4395, azstateparks.com.

Admission

Tours begin on the hour, every day, with the last one at 4:00 p.m. Tour prices for

adults and youths (7–13), $. Free admission for children 6 and under.

Events

Riordan Mansion conducts multiple events every month. A regular series of Brown Bag Lunch Lectures are offered covering a wide range of topics. High teas are held for folks who want to come dressed in their finest Edwardian or Victorian attire. Themed tours are offered during the holidays.

Picnic Area

There are picnic tables near the visitor center.

Visitor Center

Housed in the Riordan's former automotive garage, the visitor center contains some artifacts, exhibits, a video presentation, and a children's "touch table."

Nearby Attractions

Take a scenic drive north of town to visit beautiful Sunset Crater National Monument and Wupatki National Monument. The two parks are connected by a 35-mile loop road. Hundreds of volcanic craters pockmark the landscape around Flagstaff, but the baby of the bunch is the most vivid. Between 1040 and 1100, Sunset Crater blasted a geyser of molten rock and ash. The 1,000-foot-tall symmetrical cone rises above a stark landscape of cinder hills. Hike the Lava Flow Trail, a mile-long loop that curves past jagged, twisted lava slabs mingled with spatter cones and ice caves. 928-526-0502, www.nps.gov/sucr.

The dwellings of Wupatki rise like red-boned ghosts above rolling prairie. They were the work of the Ancient Pueblo people through the centuries, constructed from thin blocks of Moenkopi sandstone that give them their distinctive red color. Most were built over 900 years ago. Behind the visitor center, a self-guided paved trail curves past Wupatki Pueblo, the largest structure in the park. The sprawling three-story ruin contains nearly 100 rooms and straddles an outcropping of sandstone. 928-679-2365, www.nps.gov/wupa.

Walnut Canyon National Monument is sort of an upside-down Wupatki. Instead of being large multiroom pueblos skylined above the open prairie, the smaller dwellings of Walnut Canyon are secreted away in the natural contours of the steep-walled gorge. Protected by massive eaves of limestone, the Sinagua cliff dwellings are remarkably well preserved, and some can be entered. 928-526-3367, www.nps.gov/waca.

Slide Rock State Park

Nearest Town: Sedona.

Why Go: Visit a legendary swimming hole and natural water slide amid the red rock cliffs of Oak Creek Canyon, which proves to be stunning during every season.

This place fills me with hope. It restores a little of my faith in mankind, and that's not an easy thing to do.

By all rights, Slide Rock should have fallen by the wayside. It is a vestige of a simpler time and seems positively quaint. At heart, Slide Rock is a swimming hole. Those two words conjure up images of youthful innocence and lazy summer days.

How can a mere swimming hole compete with heated pools, water-themed megaparks, and water slides as tall as sky-scrapers? Yet Slide Rock, nestled in the heart of Oak Creek Canyon, is packed during hot weather. It's a chilly little brook, 7 miles north of Sedona, that flows through a narrow chute of smooth sandstone. And it's filled with hordes of happy, squealing kids and smiling parents.

That's what leaves me feeling hopeful. I like knowing that pleasures can still be

Slide Rock State Park is one of Arizona's legendary swimming holes. Photo by the author.

simple ones, and that the outdoors still has the power to enchant even for the most hardened couch-potato, game-glued youngsters.

Wait, There's History, Too?

Slide Rock State Park has a rich history, but that's easy to miss even though you walk right through the heart of it. From the parking lot, a wide paved path cuts across the grounds to the creek. This quarter-mile path is actually the Pendley Homestead Trail, although it's unlikely many visitors realize that. They're in a hurry and focused on cool, fast-flowing water. With barely a glance, they'll breeze past the peaceful orchards, the buildings, and an array of machinery and equipment scattered about.

Frank Pendley arrived in 1907 and

established squatter's rights at this beautiful creek-side spot. During warm months he worked the land and spent winters further south, mining and trapping bobcats. By 1910 he had figured out how to create a unique irrigation system via a series of tunnels blasted through solid rock and with flumes suspended by cables. He filed for ownership of the land under the Homestead Act and built a small cabin.

Then he set out to become a more stationary version of Johnny Appleseed, planting and tending orchards in the meadows above the creek. He experimented with several varieties of apples over the years. Red Delicious thrived, so that became the mainstay.

In 1921 Pendley married Jane Hutchinson, from another homestead in the canyon. Their house, finished in 1927, still stands, along with a 1932 apple-packing barn and a handful of tourist cabins he built in 1933 because Slide Rock was a draw even back then.

Slip Sliding Away

Of course, I get Slide Rock's popularity in the '30s. Those were hard times. Nice to be able to forget them for a while by taking a swim in a clear-running stream. Somehow Slide Rock's popularity has only grown over the ensuing decades. The Pendley family continued to operate the farm until 1985 when they sold the property to the Arizona Parklands Foundation, which in turn sold it to Arizona State Parks.

People come from all over to this unusual spot where the stone banks throttle

Now it feels like summer.
Photo by the author.

Historic orchards still grow at Slide Rock. Photo by the author.

the creek into a narrow, frothy chute that creates a natural water slide 80 feet long with a 7 percent drop from top to bottom. Algae on the rocks enhances the slipperiness. Nearby the creek widens, forming channels and pools of varying depths, perfect for wading, swimming, and cliff jumping.

Word of warning: Wear cutoffs or other sturdy shorts. It's easy to scrape bottom while zooming through the shallows, so it's not uncommon to stand up at the end of the slide only to watch big swatches of your expensive swimming suit continue downstream. And everyone should wear some kind of water shoe. Rocks are extremely slippery.

On summer days, kids and grownups alike ping-pong through the chute one after another. Downstream there's such a barrage of cannonballs it sounds like we've declared war on trout. All along the stony banks, folks sit in groups or stretch out on towels,

relaxing in the sun. In an arid landscape, water steals our hearts.

Glancing around at the idyllic little scene, it's easy to think it can't get much better than this. But that's the surprising secret of Slide Rock—it does get better. It gets better during all the other seasons.

Never an Off-Season

Show up in the spring when the orchards bloom and birds sing in the branches, or in the fall when you can buy cider and bags of fresh apples at the Slide Rock Market, or in winter when the canyon is hushed and the cliffs are frosted with snow. Show up anytime when it's too chilly to swim and your focus shifts to the jaw-dropping scenery. Slide Rock is one of the most stunning parks in the system. Everyone is just having too much fun during summer to notice.

Tall sandstone cliffs rise above the orchard and bottomland, framing the pastoral scene. These are high walls of sculpted stone, the famous red rocks of Sedona growing even more colorful and vibrant with every mood of sunlight. This segment of Oak Creek flowing over bare rock is exquisite. Without the crowds, you see every detail. Without the crowds, you hear the entire symphony—that rapturous melody of falling water played out in a chorus of minicascades.

It becomes easier to explore the park. Hike further upstream past the slide and you'll discover a shady riparian zone with trees growing on the bank and a series of ledges where you can sit and soak it all in. You can stroll through the orchards or around the homestead. Or take the quarter-mile Clifftop Nature Trail that follows the ridge overlooking the creek and includes informational signage and well-positioned benches along the way.

What becomes abundantly clear is that Slide Rock State Park is picnic nirvana. Spread across this little oasis is a ridiculous amount of prime, picnic-worthy real estate.

This is the kind of place that would have lured Yogi Bear, even if he had to kite a check to Boo-Boo for gas money. And if you're too young to get a reference to Yogi Bear and his love of pic-a-nic baskets, better bone up on cartoon history.

That's the kind of thing you have time to contemplate on a peaceful autumn day at Slide Rock while sprawled on a sunny creek-side ledge and munching a fresh-picked apple. Now it really can't get any better than this. Can it?

When You Go
Slide Rock State Park is 7 miles north of Sedona on Arizona 89A in Oak Creek Canyon. The park is day use only. Hours change seasonally. 928-282-3034, azstate parks.com.

Admission
Rates vary by season. May 26 through Labor Day: Monday through Thursday, $$ per vehicle; Friday through Sunday, $$$ per

Each season reflects a different kind of beauty at Slide Rock.
Courtesy of Mike Koopsen, Sedona.

vehicle. Tuesday after Labor Day through September 30, $$ per vehicle. October to April, $ per vehicle. May 1–25, $$ per vehicle. Up to four adults per vehicle.

Events

Fall Fest in October is the park's signature event. It celebrates the harvest with food, games, programs, apple-sorting demonstrations, and more. Vintage tractors and fly-wheelers are on display. Picnics are encouraged.

AROUND TOWN

Everybody is on the run in February for the Sedona Marathon. With races of four distances—5K, 10K, half marathon, and full marathon—lots of folks can get involved. Word around town is that if the scenery doesn't take your breath away, the hills will.

For three days in July, tiny colorful birds are the stars. The Sedona Hummingbird Festival features garden tours, hummingbird banding, informative presentations, and breakfasts at known hummer hotspots.

Park Store

The Slide Rock Market is open year-round with seasonal hours of operation. They sell snacks, hot dogs, ice cream, bottled water, books, souvenirs, and everything you need to take a swim—sunscreen, beach towels, shorts, T-shirts, hats, and aqua shoes.

Pets

Pets are not permitted in the swim area and cannot be left in the vehicle. Pets must be on a leash and attended to at all times.

Fast Fact: Pink Jeep Tours was started by a realtor who drove potential clients into the Sedona backcountry to look at property. Not many people bought but they all loved the jeep ride.

Picnic Areas

There are 15 picnic tables near the entry station. More are located in front of Slide Rock Market.

Swimming

The Slide Rock swim area is approximately a half mile of creek. There are multiple places to swim and wade, as well as the famous slide. Glass containers are prohibited in the swim area. All water-based activities are at the risk of the user. No lifeguard is on duty.

Trails

Pendley Homestead Trail is a paved 0.25-mile easy path across the former farm.

Slide Rock Route is the 0.3-mile path along the creek to the swim area.

Clifftop Nature Trail begins near the apple barn and rambles through woods overlooking the swim area. Benches are located at some of the best viewpoints.

Nearby Attractions

Ancient cultures took advantage of Sedona's abundant resources, most notably the Sinaguas, ancestors of the Hopis, who lived in the region from 1100 to 1350. They built large villages of elaborate cliff dwellings and created panels of rock art. Set against soaring magenta cliffs are the remains of two of these hamlets, Palatki and Honanki. Palatki, which means "red house" in the Hopi language, consists of two pueblos built under south-facing overhangs for shelter and the warmth of the winter sun. There's also a trail leading back to alcoves sheltering a remarkable display of pictographs, or painted symbols, adorning the rocks. Nearby Honanki, or "bear house," represents one of the largest population centers in the Verde Valley. The Forest Service limits the number of visitors, so call for reservations at 928-282-3854.

Lack of light pollution combined with

haze-free, low-humidity desert skies makes Sedona a paradise for stargazers. Evening Sky Tours, set up outside Sedona, features professional astronomers who act as guides. Attend this nighttime outing and the heavens drop right into your lap. They begin by using laser pointers to diagram an overview of the very universe. After this introduction, guests are given time on state-of-the-art telescopes to hone in on comets, planets, and galaxies. Suddenly the rings of Saturn seem close enough to slip on to your finger. www.eveningskytours.com.

With a backyard full of wild country, it's no wonder jeep tours are a cottage industry for Sedona. There are several companies to choose from but Pink Jeep Tours is the elder statesman of the lot, bouncing into the outback for more than a half century. They offer a variety of tours but the most popular is Broken Arrow, a rugged jaunt that climbs straight up the side of the famous red rocks with stunning views across Munds Mountain Wilderness. All Pink Jeep drivers are certified by the National Association of Interpreters, so beyond the thrills, the tours provide insight into the local history, geology, flora, and fauna. 800-873-3662, www.pinkadventure tours.com.

Tonto Natural Bridge State Park

Nearest Town: Payson.

Why Go: Hidden away in a slender valley, the world's largest natural travertine bridge looms above a tree-shaded stream where tunnels, caves, and colorful formations wait to be explored.

Sometimes Arizona is famous for what isn't there. The landscape boasts some of the most remarkable holes poked into the planet. There are legendary gouges in

Tonto Natural Bridge rises above Pine Creek. Courtesy of Mike Koopsen, Sedona.

Earth's fabric, such as Grand Canyon, Meteor Crater, and Tonto Natural Bridge.

Tucked away in a narrow valley between Pine and Payson, Tonto Natural Bridge may be the most unexpected. It is believed to be the largest natural travertine bridge in the world, standing 183 feet high over a 400-foot-long tunnel that measures 150 feet wide. Yet it's almost impossible to see until you're right on top of the massive span.

A Homey Hideout

Most people fleeing for their life would be too stressed to do any serious home shopping. But Scotsman David Gowan proved to be a pretty cool customer. In 1877 Apaches were chasing the prospector when he stumbled across the big natural bridge. Gowan hid in one of the caves in the tunnel for two nights. On the third day, he poked his head out, liked what he saw, and decided he had found his new home.

Despite the run-in with his neighbors, he claimed squatter's rights to the picturesque landscape.

In 1898 Gowan persuaded his nephew, David Gowan Goodfellow, to pack up his family and move from Scotland to the rugged Arizona frontier. When the Goodfellows arrived, they had to lower their possessions, down the 500-foot slopes into the valley, by ropes and burros. The family must have been happy—or maybe it was just too much work to haul everything back out—because they lived on the site until 1948.

During that time they built a comfortable home and a handful of cabins for the few hardy souls that ventured into the rugged outback to see this impressive span.

The bridge stayed in private hands until it became a state park in 1990. Improvements to the road help, but visitors still experience a sense of the remoteness that greeted early travelers. The park entrance road turns off of Arizona 260 and winds through light timber for a couple of miles before tumbling off the edge of the world. Or so it seems. The last mile drops 750 feet in elevation and is thought to be the steepest paved road in Arizona. Many visitors reach the entry station with white knuckles gripping the steering wheel and smoke rising from brake pads.

Above and Below

The big building at the entrance is the Goodfellow Lodge, originally built in the 1920s. The front room serves as a visitor center that includes a few interpretive exhibits and a small park store.

When you pull into the parking area, there's still no sign of the namesake bridge. There's just a long meadow with picnic tables scattered about and forested canyon walls rising on two sides. Keep an eye out for javelinas, frequently seen grazing on the lawn near the buildings.

Fast Fact: The javelina, also known as the collared peccary, resembles a wild boar and stands about two feet tall. They live in family groups.

The bridge is still below you at this point, spanning Pine Creek. A network of hiking trails leads to the stream at the bottom of the gorge, but you don't have to be a hiker for a peek at the bridge. The park has created four topside viewpoints at the parking-lot level. Each offers a unique perspective of the geological wonder. All four are wheelchair accessible.

I enjoyed the fine vistas but I was here for the trails. There are four, ranging from 300 feet to a half mile. They're short but scenic and all have some steepness involved. I started with the only one that doesn't descend all the way to the creek.

The Waterfall Trail leads down a set of steps into the woods and passes a wall of gnawed travertine. It ends at a ridiculously lush little grotto of moss-covered rocks, sporting a hanging garden of ferns, columbine, and a tangle of wild blackberries. Every leaf, bloom, and berry drip with water from the cascade spilling down the cliff. The grotto is blindingly green, possibly the greenest spot in all Arizona. It looks like a hideout for leprechauns.

Thoroughly refreshed from the cool spray, I next climbed down the Gowan Trail for the classic view of the bridge. The pathway clambers down the hill, crosses a bridge, and ends at an observation deck at the mouth of the tunnel. This is where you begin to appreciate the immense size of the span. You can see caves, curious formations, and massive boulders within. A thin veil of water plunges from the top of the tunnel 200 feet in a straight drop, splashing into the creek near the deck.

I climbed out to enjoy a little lunch topside. Then it was back into the gorge, this time descending on the Anna Mae Trail, which put me on the banks of the creek on the backside of the tunnel, away from the waterfall. Some rock hopping got me beneath the bridge. In the shade of the tunnel, I saw caves and alcoves pockmarking the walls and long travertine shelves. Travertine is a form of limestone deposited by mineral-laden water. Through this big, soft rock, Pine Creek has eroded a massive passageway.

Up the Creek

It occurred to me that I wanted to see more of the feisty little stream. The natural bridge gets all the accolades, but Pine Creek did all the heavy lifting in forming it. This little waterway is the real hidden gem of the park.

I worked my way upstream, past the Anna Mae junction, along the bank, beneath overhangs, and through slender corridors of travertine. This is part of the Pine Creek Trail, but I found no clear pathway at this point. It was just me picking my way over rocks and around tree roots. I inched along because I wanted to savor all of it. Despite the number of people at the bridge, I had this riparian corridor all to myself.

Shafts of sunlight pierced the leaf canopy and danced on the water. In typical Arizona fashion, the stream maintains only a stuttering flow. It's mostly a series of pools and drops, linked by a thin silver thread. The splashy music of fountains and cascades echoed through the trees. This stretch of canyon bottom was a sweet oasis for me.

After I followed the water for several hundred feet, the trail branched to the right, climbing through the woods back to the parking lot. There was a nice crowd of

---

Fast Fact: Most natural bridges are sandstone or hard limestone.

Historic Goodfellow Lodge has been lovingly restored. Courtesy of Arizona State Parks and Trails, Phoenix.

visitors at the park. We all saw the geological wonder that is Tonto Natural Bridge. But it felt like I was the only one who got the whole story.

When You Go

Tonto Natural Bridge State Park is located 14 miles northwest of Payson off Arizona 260. The park is open from 9:00 a.m. to 6:00 p.m. Last entry is at 5:00 p.m. 928-476-4202, azstateparks.com.

Admission

Adults and youths (7–13), $. Free admission for children 6 and under.

Goodfellow Lodge

The three-story, cabin-style lodge has been restored and is available to rent for special occasions like weddings and family reunions. It comes with 10 furnished bedrooms with private and communal restrooms, and includes the ADA-accessible Roosevelt Suite. There's a large kitchen and dining area with picnic-table seating. Currently, the lodge is only available for group rentals, although that may change in the future. Maximum occupancy is 28 people.

Picnic Areas

There are several picnic tables scattered among the trees surrounding the lodge and parking area, above the natural bridge.

Swimming

No swimming is permitted under the natural bridge. Swimming is allowed downstream in Pine Creek. As always, use caution. There is no lifeguard on duty, and swimming is at your own risk.

Trails

Gowan Trail is a steep trail about 2200 feet long leading to an observation deck in the creek bottom.

Anna Mae Trail (500 feet) descends steeply to the canyon bottom on the backside of the natural bridge and connects to Pine Creek Trail.

At a half mile, Pine Creek Trail is the longest route in the park, through woods into the canyon and along the creek bottom. Arrows are painted on rocks at the creek to aid navigation.

Waterfall Trail is about 300 feet long, down a series of uneven stairs through dense undergrowth and ending at a waterfall cave.

Pets and glass containers are prohibited on the trails. There is no public telephone, cell phone signal, or internet access in the park.

Visitor Center

Located in the Goodfellow Lodge, the visitor center features artifacts and interpretive exhibits on the history of the natural bridge and the lodge, along with a small park store.

Nearby Attractions

Built of pine logs in 1885 and opened the following year, the rustic, one-room Strawberry Schoolhouse looks like it would easily qualify as the oldest schoolhouse still standing in Arizona. It often gets touted that way. And it would be, except for the one in Arivaca that dates back to 1879. But this one is still very cool and now serves as an informative little museum, complete with a late nineteenth-century classroom exhibit. Located on Fossil Creek Road in Strawberry (west of Arizona 87), the schoolhouse is open on weekends from mid-May through mid-October. The small but charming hamlets of Pine and Strawberry are just a few miles north of the park and well worth a visit.

The Shoofly Village Ruin is what remains of a community occupied from AD 1000 to 1250 by as many as 250 people. A self-guided walking tour loops through the four-acre site past low rock walls and crumbling courtyards. Interpretive signs offer visitors a glimpse into the prehistoric community. Shoofly Village is located just off Houston Mesa Road in Payson, about 3 miles north of Arizona 87. Picnic tables and restrooms are available.

At Rim Country Museum you get a great history lesson in a lakeside setting. The museum occupies an old forest ranger station and contains a wealth of artifacts and exhibits reflecting the early history of the region, including the savage Pleasant Valley War, the bloodiest feud of the American West. Admission price includes a guided tour through the museum and the Zane Grey Cabin, which was re-created after the original cabin of the Western writer was lost in a 1990 fire. Best of all, the museums are perched on a shady hill overlooking three lakes in Green Valley Park. 700 South Green Valley Parkway, 928-474-3483, www.rimcountrymuseum.org.

SOUTHERN ARIZONA PARKS

Southern Arizona State Parks

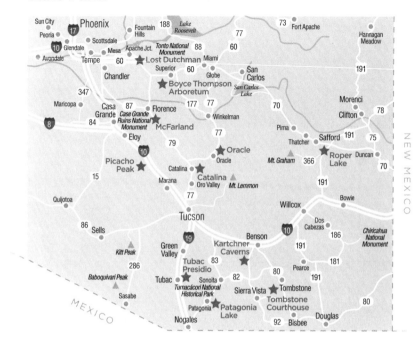

MEXICO

AMENITIES IN SOUTHERN ARIZONA STATE PARKS

Tubac Presidio	Courthouse	Tombstone	Roper Lake	Picacho Peak	Patagonia Lake	Oracle	McFarland	Lost Dutchman	Caverns	Kartchner	Catalina	Boyce Thompson	PARKS
			•	•									BOATING
										•	•		CABINS
			•	•						•	•		CAMPING
			•										FISHING
•			•	•	•	•		•	•		•	•	HIKING
•	•											•	HISTORIC BUILDINGS
						•	•				•		MOUNTAIN BIKING
•		•	•	•	•	•		•			•	•	PICNIC AREAS
•		•	•	•	•	•			•		•	•	PROGRAMS
			•	•									SWIMMING

Picket Post House, built in the 1920s, overlooks Boyce Thompson Arboretum. Courtesy of Rick Mortensen, Cincinnati.

Boyce Thompson Arboretum State Park

Nearest Town: Superior.
Why Go: Arizona's oldest and largest arboretum offers a peaceful sanctuary where desert plants from around the world fill lavish gardens at the base of Picketpost Mountain.

At Boyce Thompson Arboretum, expect the unexpected. This is a fanciful place full of surprises, a place where the comings and goings of buzzards prompt a party, where odd-looking trees leap off the pages of fiction and take root. They have a creek but it mostly flows underground. Endangered fish swim in a lake that shouldn't exist. Autumn puts on a brilliant display of colorful leaves but not until winter is knocking on the door. Herbs and flowers grow like weeds. Meanwhile, there are no weeds. There's a big house built on a hill and a little house built under a cliff. And my favorite exhibit is a rusted pickup truck with flat tires and a cactus growing in the bed.

Yard Gone Wild

Colonel William Boyce Thompson, a wealthy mining engineer, founded the arboretum in the 1920s. While working as a Red Cross leader in Russia during World War I, Thompson developed an appreciation of plants as a source of food, clothing, and shelter. He decided then to apply his wealth to improve the use of plant resources.

It's always nice to hear about a rich guy

who does positive things with his bankroll, no matter how offbeat. I like to envision the colonel enjoying a beverage in his neighborhood saloon (or depending on the year, speakeasy) and suddenly slapping the bar with his hand and yelling, "Cactus for everybody!"

He went on a spending spree, purchasing drought-tolerant plants for his Arizona property. That yard continued to grow and today encompasses 392 acres, making it the state's largest and oldest botanical garden.

Over 4,000 different types of plants from the deserts of Australia, North and South America, Africa, and other arid regions are spread across the landscape at the base of Picketpost Mountain. More than 3 miles of trails weave through the themed gardens. Boyce Thompson Arboretum became part of the University of Arizona in 1965 and is now in the College of Agriculture and Life Sciences. In 1976 it became part of the Arizona State Parks system.

A Forest in the Desert

Set aside any notion you might have of the desert being stark. Boyce Thompson is a shady sanctuary, a peaceful oasis where cacti rub spiny elbows with a stunning collection of drought-tolerant trees, including eucalyptus, sycamore, black walnut, hackberry, soapberry, and Chinese pistachio. It's the latter that adds an extension to the fall color display, turning bright hues of orange and red in late November into early December.

Of course, the most intriguing tree

Fast Fact: William Thompson also founded the Boyce Thompson Institute for plant research in Yonkers, New York, now affiliated with Cornell University. Thompson expected the institute to make valuable contributions to general scientific knowledge, biology, and medicine.

---

contributes no shade or colorful leaves but it will likely put a smile on your face. The boojum tree looks like an upside-down parsnip in need of a shave. The stiff, upward-tapering trunk bristles with short, slender branches and small leaves that generally drop off during warm weather. The name comes from the mythical Boojum featured in Lewis Carroll's poem "The Hunting of the Snark."

The Main Trail makes a 1.5-mile loop through the arboretum. It's a wide, smooth path suitable for wheelchairs, at least until you reach Ayer Lake. (The Demonstration Garden, the Hummingbird and Butterfly Garden, and the Children's Garden are also wheelchair accessible.) Tucked at the base of a ridge of ragged, jagged bare rock and fringed by cattails, Ayer Lake is home for the desert pupfish and the Gila topminnow. They're both endangered species but are living large in this desert pond. Arizona Game and Fish uses this population to restock other bodies of water where the fish have died off.

Past Ayer Lake, the Main Trail makes a steeper, twisting climb amid thrusts of eerie stone columns and towers, the remnants of ancient volcanic ash. That imposing mansion perched on the high ledge overhead is the Picket Post House. It was built from 1923 to 1924 and used as a winter home by Colonel Thompson.

The trail descends from the ridge to the banks above Queen Creek. Like many streams in Arizona, Queen Creek is a part-timer. It normally runs in the winter months and again following summer storms. The rest of the time it flows underground.

Not-So-Secret Gardens

The Cactus and Succulent Garden showcases over 300 species while the Taylor Legume Garden highlights plants from the pea family. Stop by the Herb Garden for the sweet fragrance and to marvel at the Clevenger House, a small stone structure tucked partially beneath a large rock overhang. It's the kind of tiny house that excites downsizing hipsters. Wonder if Clevenger knew how trendy it would become when he and the wife were raising three kids under the little roof.

Half-pints can explore a maze, dig for buried treasure, and find plenty of other ways to get dirty in the Children's Garden. Their parents can glean some landscape ideas from the Demonstration Garden, which happens to be one of the most serene and tranquil corners of the arboretum. I like to sit quietly and listen to the splash of fountains and watch the colorful ballet of butterflies and hummingbirds swarming above the flowering plants.

Yet my favorite spot is hidden away in the Australian Desert. Deep in the shade of eucalyptus trees, surrounded by plants from the Land Down Under, stands a rickety shack, built to resemble a drover's wool shed. It's a peaceful albeit ramshackle camp, and parked in the yard is a beautiful old 1957 Dodge Power Wagon. The rusted pickup has nothing whatsoever to do with Australia, yet it steals the scene. I am a sucker for old trucks.

The Dodge was bought new by the arboretum, a very large purchase for a foundation always scrambling for funds. It proved to be a workhorse and lasted into the 1990s. As the decades passed, replacement parts became impossible to find. Near the end it was confined to the arboretum property since the brakes no longer worked. Drivers would have to open the door and drag their feet to cruise to a stop, Fred Flintstone style.

Finally, after a solemn ceremony, the ancient truck was retired and added to the Aussie exhibit. In the bed are a few bales of hay and a growing prickly-pear cactus, one final load ready for delivery.

School's Never Out

A place this special wins many fans. Swarms of volunteers have become an invaluable resource, constantly weeding, planting, and pruning, then weeding some more. They also act as docents conducting tours and workshops throughout the year.

It's not just plants they're teaching about. Such an oasis is bound to attract abundant wildlife. More than 300 species of birds, reptiles, amphibians, and mammals reside in the park. Plenty more are frequent visitors.

Bird walks are regular events but so are dragonfly walks, butterfly walks, and lizard workshops. A flock of turkey vultures shows up each March and departs in September, and the arboretum throws a bash for each occurrence.

Programs on geology, history, photography, and botany fill out the schedule. They even hold a book club with lively discussions. Beyond the beauty, education is the emphasis at Boyce Thompson Arboretum. Somewhere, Colonel Thompson has to be smiling.

Cactus for everybody!

When You Go

Boyce Thompson Arboretum is located 3 miles west of Superior, 55 miles east of Phoenix at 37615 East US 60. It is open from 8:00 a.m. to 5:00 p.m. October through April, and 6:00 a.m. to 3:00 p.m. May through September. Last admission is one hour prior to closing. 602-827-3000, azstateparks.com, www.btarboretum.org.

Admission

Adults $$, youths (5–12) $.

Events

The arboretum offers a series of programs and events, most of them included in the park admission price. There's an Australia Day in January, a Welcome Back Buzzards

Ayer Lake adds a welcome bit of water to the desert landscape of Boyce Thompson Arboretum. Courtesy of Rick Mortensen, Cincinnati.

festival in mid-March, seasonal plant sales in March and October, a Bye-Bye Buzzards Day in September, and a Fall Color Festival on Thanksgiving weekend.

Seasonally appropriate weekend tours take place throughout the year. They include bird, butterfly, dragonfly, and lizard walks. There is a Plants of the Bible Land Walking Tour, an Edible and Medicinal Plants Walk, and a Tuesday Book Club. There are history, geology, photography, and botany tours; pottery classes, pomegranate-harvest workshops, master gardener workshops, prickly-pear fruit classes, and . . . well, you get the idea. Consult the website for a complete listing of events or call the park.

Membership

Become a member of the arboretum and receive an array of benefits such as free admission for a year, guest passes, discounts on purchases and special classes, and a member newsletter.

Picnic Area

There are several tables and charcoal grills in the picnic area near the Demonstration Garden.

Trails

Besides the 1.5-mile Main Trail, there are several other paths that loop through various gardens. The High Trail offers slightly more of a challenge than the others as it traces a ridgeline on the south bank of Queen Creek. It's only 0.45 miles but there are some stairs to negotiate and uneven rocky surfaces. The views up the canyon are spectacular.

Despite the fact that the trails are short, allow yourself plenty of time to finish. This is a park to spend time savoring the details. Signs are posted on trails that are not recommended for wheelchairs.

Visitor Center

Admission is collected and information is provided at the visitor center, which also serves as a gift shop and plant store. Books, artwork, gifts, and souvenirs are available inside, and the patio is filled with plants for sale. You'll find cacti, agaves, aloes, trees, shrubs, herbs, and flowers, so you can work some of the arboretum magic in your own yard. Plants are sold year-round and a larger selection is available during seasonal plant-sale fundraisers in March and October.

Nearby Attractions

Robert Taylor Jones arrived in the Arizona Territory in 1909 and settled in Superior. He became a pharmacist before entering politics, serving as state senator, and he was elected as Arizona's sixth governor from 1939 to 1940. His former Superior home, shaded by big palm trees, is now the Bob Jones Museum. It features artifacts and photos detailing the history of the region and the mining industry, as well as a diorama of the nearby ghost town of Pinal City. 300 Main Street, 520-689-1969.

The World's Smallest Museum in Superior was built in the mid-1990s as a way to lure diners into the Buckboard City Cafe, right next door. And it packs an interesting oddball collection of stuff into its 134 square feet of space. Exhibits are set behind glass panels and include a hodgepodge of stuff such as vinyl records, an old typewriter, a Beatles concert poster, ore samples from nearby mines, and surprisingly for a self-proclaimed world's smallest place, the world's largest Apache tear. The museum is free and open during café hours. 1111 West US Highway 60, 520-689-5800.

Catalina State Park

Nearest Town: Tucson.
Why Go: The Santa Catalina Mountains form a dramatic skyline above this desert park veined with trails open to hikers, mountain bikers, and equestrians.

If they ever let me design a state park, it would probably look very much like Catalina.

Beautiful desert, soaring mountains, miles of hiking trails, historic sites, wildflowers, occasional water, bighorn sheep, and ice cream—that's pretty much my entire wish list. And Catalina checks all the boxes.

The 5,500-acre park spreads across the foothills and canyons of the mighty Santa Catalina Mountains, commonly referred to as the Catalina Mountains, just north of Tucson. This pristine swath of desert was once in the cross hairs of developers but thank heavens wiser heads prevailed.

Catalina is a pull-you-outside kind of park. There's a great mix of trails, not just for hikers but also for mountain bikers and equestrians. There are a few short, gentle ones for folks who just want to stretch their legs and maybe do a little birding or study some ancient ruins. Moderate trails provide a workout and show off some of the best scenery Tucson has to offer and that's saying a lot. Then there are hard-core routes that exit the park and continue on to the adjacent Coronado National Forest, the Pusch Ridge Wilderness, and the highest elevations of the Santa Catalinas.

Pick your adventure.

Tucson's Santa Catalina Mountains form the rugged backdrop for Catalina State Park. Courtesy of Rick Mortensen, Cincinnati.

Hard Times

Driving into the park, the first trail you'll spot is to Romero Ruins. This is a good introduction, an easy 0.75-mile loop that crosses a wash, then climbs a low hill where you'll find the remains of a Hohokam village dating back to about AD 500. You'll have to use your imagination for most of it, aided by some interpretive signage that tells you what you're looking at.

There are some more distinctive rock walls amid the chollas and prickly pears but these are the footprints of a homestead built by Francisco Romero before 1850. This is a picturesque but lonely spot for a ranch and Romero was the target of many Apache raids. It's likely that he cannibalized some of the stone walls built by the Hohokam to shore up his own defenses. Rangers often lead guided hikes here.

All the other trails (with the exception of the 50-Year Trail) leave from the trailhead. Continue to follow the main park road until it ends. This is the trailhead, with pathways gathered in a convenient cluster. There's a big parking area, restrooms, picnic tables, and a small store that operates during the busy season. One of the great pleasures of hiking at Catalina (at least for me) is that you can walk off a trail and then stop by the store to snag a cold treat. You can actually be eating ice cream before you get back in your car! If that's not a great hiking day, I don't what is.

Boots on the Ground

The Birding Trail and Nature Trail are both easy 1-mile loops that give you a chance to enjoy fun-size bites of desert. Informational signs are posted along the Nature Trail, if you want to exercise your brain along with your legs. I recommend Canyon Loop because it curves through the foothills, with stunning mountain vistas. The easy hike (2.3 miles) stays mostly level except for one slope of 90 stairs. It rambles through big stands of saguaro and crosses a wide sandy wash a few times. So if you're fortunate to be here when water is flowing, you might get to rock hop or splash across.

Canyon Loop passes the junction with Sutherland Trail. This is another gem, especially in spring. The best wildflower displays in Catalina State Park can be found on the first mile or so of the Sutherland Trail. Fields of poppies streak the desert following wet winters, along with a supporting cast of lupines, globe mallows, desert chicories, creamcups, and more.

The Sutherland requires discipline because you'll need to stop and turn yourself around at some point, unless you're prepared for a grueling 18+ miles on the trail. The first few miles are easy enough, with beautiful mountain views. The Sutherland eventually leaves the park, entering the Coronado National Forest, the Desert Bighorn Sheep Management Area, and the wilderness area. It makes a rocky ascent and ends after 9.1 miles at the Mount Lemmon Trail. No dogs are allowed in the bighorn management area and no bikes in the wilderness.

The Romero Canyon Trail rambles for a moderate mile to the Montrose Pools (usually dry) and the park boundary. The next 1.8 miles are a steeper, rockier climb but come with a nice payoff when you reach the Romero Pools, sheltered ponds fed by small cascades in a bare rock defile. It's a refreshing end to a hot, shadeless hike.

The same rules apply to Romero Canyon—no dogs, no bikes, and it's not recommended for horses beyond Montrose Pools.

Every trail offers the savory blend that makes Catalina State Park so beloved. Clusters of towering saguaros are set against a skyline of mountains that are a combination of the Rockies and something out of J. R. R. Tolkien's Middle-earth. The Santa Catalinas have an almost pastoral feel on the lower slopes clad in mesquite bosques and desert scrub, but their upper reaches are sheer domes and savage cliffs. I kept scanning the high ground for orcs.

Climbing the Walls

The first 30 desert bighorn sheep were reintroduced into the Pusch Ridge Wilderness

on the cliffs above the park in 2013. The eventual goal is to establish a herd of 100. So far, so good. In 2014 a pair of lambs was sighted, the first bighorn sheep born in the Catalina Mountains in almost 25 years.

The bighorn seem to be doing well enough that you may not have to make a steep climb in hopes of spotting one. They occasionally show up within Catalina State Park boundaries.

Desert bighorn are native to the Southwest, but populations declined drastically with the arrival of European settlers. Conservation efforts to reestablish populations in suitable habitats have improved the fortunes of the big, stocky sheep. Their concave, elastic hooves and keen eyesight allow them to traverse impossibly steep rocky terrain.

If you've never seen bighorn sheep cavorting on their home turf, it is

Arizona State Parks can be explored in a variety of ways. Photo by the author.

Most trails in Catalina State Park are open to hikers, equestrians, and mountain bikers. Courtesy of Arizona State Parks and Trails, Phoenix.

astonishing. I witnessed this with the first one I ever encountered. I was hiking deep in the Grand Canyon and rounded a bend on the South Kaibab Trail and there was a bighorn. For an instant, I was thrilled at a new animal sighting. But that quickly turned to shock when I watched the young ram plunge to his death.

Or that's what it seemed. As soon as he spotted me, he leapt off the trail into the abyss. I thought, "Good lord, I've driven the beast to suicide." Except, instead of falling hundreds of feet, he landed on a pencil eraser–sized rock 10 feet from the edge, and without slowing down, made his next leap to another ridiculous landing spot, and another, and went zigzagging down the sheer canyon wall.

So when you're hiking in Catalina marveling at the scenery, keep an eye peeled for the sure-footed critters clambering about. That kind of sighting would be a sweet bonus for any park visit.

When You Go

Catalina State Park sits at the base of the Santa Catalina Mountains 9 miles north of Tucson. 11570 North Oracle Road, 520-628-5798, azstateparks.com.

Admission

$ per vehicle (up to four adults).

Biking

Cycling is permitted on all trails except Romero Ruin Interpretive Trail.

Camping

The campgrounds have 120 electric and water sites for both tent and RV camping. All sites offer a picnic table and barbecue grill. There is no limit on the length of RVs.

Equestrian Area

An equestrian staging area and camping area is available for visitors who trailer their own livestock. Stock can be off-loaded for day rides, or riders can camp with their animals. 16 pens are available first-come, first-served at no charge. Picnic tables, BBQ grills, restrooms, and drinking water are available. Horses are not permitted on the Nature Trail, Birding Trail, or Romero Ruin Interpretive Trail, or in picnic/camping areas or on paved roads. Camping fees apply.

Events

Guided hikes, star parties, and First Saturday concerts are regular events at Catalina State Park.

Picnic Areas

The shady picnic area is adjacent to the trailhead and features tables, BBQ grills, and restrooms.

Trailhead Store

Besides the store at the Visitor Center, the trailhead gift shop is open seasonally, selling various necessary items, including ice cream.

Trails

In addition to those already described, the easy Bridle Trail (1.4 miles) connects the Equestrian Center with the trailhead. The 50-Year Trail (8.6 miles) is especially popular with equestrians and mountain bikers because it follows a ridgeline out of the park and into open desert. The 2.2-mile Trail Link connects the 50-Year Trail with the Sutherland. All trails are multiuse except Romero Ruin.

Nearby Attractions

Two sections of Saguaro National Park bookend Tucson and create a genuine backcountry that laps at residents' doorsteps. On the east side of town, the Rincon Mountain District of Saguaro NP contains the scenic Cactus Forest Drive. This one-way paved loop road curves through a bristling grove of saguaros. A series of interconnected trails branch off from the road, so you can get out and ramble among the tall, lanky cacti. The Tucson Mountain District (the west unit) features multiple trails, including Signal Hill, which makes an easy climb to ancient petroglyphs. 520-733-5153, www.nps.gov/sagu.

Stop for a stroll on Fourth Avenue, Tucson's most eclectic shopping district. Bookstores rub shoulders with vintage-clothing shops and art galleries. You'll find everything from recycled toys to unique jewelry, home decor, and gifts from Nepal tucked between ethnic eateries and bars. Located between University Boulevard and Ninth Avenue. www.fourthavenue.org.

Tucson Botanical Gardens is a place of beauty and inspiration with a little education slyly mixed in. This nonprofit oasis shows homeowners the endless possibilities and myriad looks of desert plants. The 17 display gardens are packed into just 5.5 acres of land. As you move from the Zen garden to the wildflower garden to the butterfly greenhouse to Aloe Alley, you develop a whole new appreciation of desert plants. 2150 North Alvernon Way, 520-326-9686, tucsonbotanical.org.

Kartchner Caverns State Park

Nearest town: Benson.

Why Go: Tour a living, breathing limestone cave adorned with a breathtaking array of formations including stalagmites, stalactites, soda straws, and helictites.

Nothing really prepares you for the details of the subterranean architecture. It's a dazzling display of limestone temples and cathedrals of calcite. Towers and columns, spikes and spires—these give structure to the immense space. This is Atlantis. This is

El Dorado and Moria. This is the stuff of lost cities.

Turn the Grand Canyon inside out and you have Kartchner Caverns.

The stunning cave lies hidden beneath the rough hills of the Whetstone Mountains in southeastern Arizona. Kartchner is a wet, living cave with water still percolating down from the surface and formations still growing. A bristling forest of stalactites, stalagmites, columns, and crystals fills the soaring rooms. Pencil-thin soda straws dangle from the ceiling, including one of the longest in the world at 21 feet and 3 inches.

In 2016 Kartchner Caverns was voted the best cave in the United States by a *USA*

Fast Fact: A drop of water that falls on a visitor is called a "cave kiss."

Today reader poll. The story of how the underground caverns became a state park is almost as impressive as the wonders found within.

A Brief History

Randy Tufts and Gary Tenen were a couple of young cavers poking around in the foothills of the Whetstones in 1974 when they noticed a gush of warm, moist air emanating from a sinkhole. Squeezing through a narrow crack near the bottom and crawling for several hundred yards, they found a

Formations are still growing and developing in Kartchner Caverns.
Courtesy of Arizona State Parks and Trails, Phoenix.

spectacular pristine cave, one that showed no signs of human presence.

For four years Tufts and Tenen kept their discovery a closely guarded secret. They knew if word leaked out, curious visitors would irreparably damage the cave. After finding out everything they could about the Kartchner family who owned the land, the cavers took them into their confidence in 1978. All agreed that the caverns must be protected and they plotted how best to do that.

Finally, in 1984 the group approached a representative of Arizona State Parks. Everything was done under a cloak of secrecy, including blindfolding state officials before taking them to the cave. The agency acquired the land in 1988. Over the next decade, $28 million was put into the careful development of Kartchner Caverns. It opened to the public in 1999.

Going Underground

Visitors who are signed up for one of the guided tours of Kartchner are shuttled via electric trams from the Discovery Center into the hills to the cavern entrance. No more slithering in like reptiles. Now entry is through impressive NORAD-style air locks and beneath a row of misters to damp down any dust and lint that we might be transporting. This is all done to preserve the essential humidity of the caverns and to protect its delicate features.

The cave has an average temperature of 72 degrees Fahrenheit and 99 percent humidity year-round. The wall of moist air throws an embrace around you as soon as

---

Fast Fact: No one knows where the bats go when they leave Kartchner Caverns, but it is suspected that they hibernate over the winter in a cold cave high in the Huachuca Mountains about 40 miles away.

---

you enter. The occasional drip of water echoes in the stillness.

It feels like walking into the chambers of a beating heart.

Wide concrete trails with handrails weave through the spacious rooms. There are only a few areas with slightly steep grades that may require extra help for someone in a wheelchair. Benches are available along the way.

Two guided tours, the Rotunda/Throne Tour and the Big Room Tour, are offered most days and are both spectacular. Each tour covers a half mile, although the trek to the Big Room is slightly longer. The Big Room is closed from mid-April through mid-October so the resident bats can return and give birth.

In 2014 the Helmet and Headlamp Tour was added, and that's become one of my favorite ways to explore the cave.

The Wonder of Light and Dark

Once we passed through the air-lock doors and proceeded down the tunnel, all lights in the cave were turned off. We entered seeing the exotic formations in the glow of our bobbing headlamps. The enormity of the caverns was revealed little by little. A ranger led and another brought up the rear. While we were still closely monitored—no touching anything but the handrail—there was a comfortable looseness to the tour. The rangers provided a little information but spent most of the time answering questions or just stepping back and allowing us to savor plenty of quiet wonder.

Of course, some of us had more specific goals. The youngest member of our group could be heard muttering "bacon, bacon, bacon" under his breath. He was a single-minded cute kid. "Bacon, bacon, bacon!"

Cave bacon is a type of flowstone formed when water runs down a wall or along a ledge, depositing calcite along a thin ridge. Over time the ridge continues to grow with

Fast Fact: Stalactites are formations that hang from the ceiling of caves. Stalagmites rise from the ground.

folds and kinks. The changing mineral composition of the water adds bands of color until the rock looks freakishly like strips of delicious bacon.

It's one of several subterranean formations named for food, along with cave popcorn, fried-egg stalagmites, and soda straws. My theory is that cavers crawl around in cramped, dark places and spend a lot of time thinking about their next meal until even the rocks look edible.

We moved slowly, focused on whatever caught our fancy. We lingered often and enjoyed some perks denied to regular tours. In the Strawberry Room, we were escorted into a small cordoned-off alcove to study the ceiling shaggy with stalactites, slender soda straws, and the gnarled, twisted witch fingers of helictites.

At another point, we all took seats on a stone bench and clicked off our headlamps. Midnight in ninja pajamas abruptly dropped in our laps. If you've never experienced total darkness, it's disconcerting in a slightly joyful way. You have to blink occasionally just to remind yourself that your eyes are open. We sat for several minutes in giggly awe. Many of us allegedly waved hands in front of faces but there was no way to prove it. Without a speck of light, absolutely nothing can be seen. It's a rare experience and was the part of the tour that many in our group found the most memorable.

Yet for me, the most unforgettable moment was as I stood in the Cul de Sac Passageway. The group was strung out a bit, each focused on different areas. I was scanning the ceiling, my headlamp sweeping across the jagged protrusions, and I noticed dozens of glistening crystals. It took me a

minute to realize that these were all single drops of water still clinging to the tips of the stalactites above.

I was witnessing the process. These tiny wet diamonds were what created and decorated this elaborate cavern. Water seeps into a limestone cave, drips from the ceiling, and leaves behind a microscopic dab of dissolved chemicals. That residue left after each drip accumulates, slowly growing into a formation. Scientists estimate that it would take more than 750 years to accumulate one inch of solid material. The trajectory of the water and the type of minerals carried by the water account for the varied colors and formations found. That includes cave bacon, which, according to the rangers, excites virtually every kid who visits Kartchner.

Standing there in the shadows, I felt like I was part of a cosmic patience. Ancient this place might be, but thoroughly modern, too. The cave is still being formed. The process is allowed to continue. It was given that chance because the two young guys who found it wanted to do the right thing and so did everyone else that got involved.

To assure your spot, reserve cave-tour tickets online for Kartchner Caverns. Courtesy of Arizona State Parks and Trails, Phoenix.

It's not just what's underground—Kartchner Caverns has been designated as an International Dark Sky Park. Courtesy of Arizona State Parks and Trails, Phoenix.

That's a story you don't hear too often anymore.

Also, the kid is right. I could totally go for some bacon about now.

When You Go

Kartchner Caverns State Park is located near Benson on Arizona 90, 9 miles south of Exit 302 off I-10. The park entrance gate is closed from 10:00 p.m. to 6:00 a.m. 520-586-4100, azstateparks.com.

Admission

$ per vehicle (up to four adults). The fee is waived for people with cave-tour or campsite reservations.

Cabins

The campground features four heated, air-conditioned cabins with queen bed, two sets of bunk beds, a table, chairs, a microwave, a minifridge, and a covered wooden porch. Bring your own bedding or sleeping bags, towels, utensils, and so on. And pack a flashlight for nighttime walks to the restrooms and showers.

Camping

All 58 sites have electricity hookups. There are picnic tables, showers, flush toilets, and a dump station.

Dark Skies

Kartchner Caverns has been designated an International Dark Sky Park. It is one of two state parks in Arizona to receive the recognition from the International Dark-Sky Association (the other is Oracle State Park). Star parties with astronomy clubs setting up telescopes for celestial viewing are wildly popular events. Of course, folks spending the night at the park at other times have the heavens all to themselves.

Events

Once each month the caverns offer a special tour allowing guests to take photos inside the cave. Star parties and guided hikes occur throughout the year.

Picnic Areas

Several shaded picnic tables are located around the perimeter of the main parking area and adjacent to the café. There are wheelchair-accessible tables with parking.

Tours

Cave-tour reservations are available online or by calling 877-MY-PARKS.

The Rotunda/Throne Tour examines the role water plays in creating the caverns. It highlights the original trail pioneered by Tenen and Tufts, and plenty of colorful formations, including Kubla Khan, a massive 58-foot column. The tour ends with a striking light and sound show. The tour covers a half mile and lasts 90 minutes. $$$ for adults, $$ for children 7–13, $ for kids under 7.

The Big Room Tour also takes in a wide range of decorations, but the talk emphasizes cave fauna, living and ancient, and discusses Kartchner's resident bat population. It lasts an hour and 45 minutes. Big Room Tours are not available for children under the age of 7. $$$ for adults, and $$ for children 7–13.

Reservations should always be made in advance. Please arrive at least an hour before your scheduled tour time. Late arrival may result in the forfeiture of your tour slot.

Helmet and Headlamp Tours are offered only on Saturdays, after other tours have finished for the day, so that the lights can be turned off. Tours last an hour and 15 minutes. From October through April, tours are held in the Big Room. The rest of the year they follow the Rotunda/Throne

route. The cost is $$$, and no children under 10 are allowed.

No items are allowed into the cave. That means no bags, purses, cameras, cell phones, packs, bottled water, strollers, walkers, crutches, etc. Lockers are available to store your items. Wheelchairs and motorized scooters are permitted in the cave, but there are some restrictions on size. Manual wheelchairs are available for loan. Canes with rubber tips are also allowed.

Trails

A short nature walk introduces visitors to local vegetation. Three hiking trails traverse the park. The moderate Foothills Loop makes a 2.5-mile swing through the limestone hills that shelter the caverns. The Ocotillo Trail (1.7 miles) can be accessed from the Foothills Loop and rambles to a saddle with expansive views of the San Pedro River Valley, continuing up a steep hillside after that point. The Guindani Trail, 4.2 miles, climbs from desert grasslands to oak-juniper woodlands on the higher slopes of the Whetstone Mountains. It's rated easy for the first mile but becomes more strenuous after that.

Visitor Center

The spacious Discovery Center features an interactive museum with fun and educational displays. This is a good place to handle the rocks and formations and get that out of your system. Inside the cave, touching is strictly forbidden. There's a theater where a 15-minute movie is shown featuring Tenen and Tufts telling the story of finding and protecting the cave. There's also a well-stocked gift shop.

The Bat Cave Café serves sandwiches, hot dogs, quesadillas, muffins, and more. Besides patio seating in the hummingbird garden, several shaded picnic tables are available.

Nearby Attractions

Gammons Gulch is a re-created Western town sitting on 10 acres amid rolling desert hills north of Benson. It was built to serve as a movie set and living museum and is stocked with an intriguing mix of Hollywood memorabilia and historic artifacts. Every building is a gem, many constructed from salvaged materials. You'll find doors from Wyatt Earp–era Tombstone, some still with original wavy glass panels. Owner Jay Gammons offers informative, funny tours for visitors, providing the stories behind his impressive collection. Call ahead to make sure tours are scheduled. 520-212-2831, gammonsgulch.com.

The San Pedro River supports some of the richest wildlife habitat in the Southwest as it meanders north from Mexico to join the Gila River. The San Pedro Riparian National Conservation Area shelters 57,000 acres of cottonwood-willow forest, mesquite bosques, and marshy ciénagas, as well as multiple historic sites. The San Pedro House, a 1930s-era converted ranch building, serves as bookstore and visitor center, and makes a great access point for hikers and birders east of Sierra Vista. 9800 Arizona 90, 520-508-4445, sanpedroriver.org/wpfspr.

Fairbank is a ghost town with meat on its bones. A half-dozen structures—including a large mercantile building, a schoolhouse, and a few homes—huddle amid riverside mesquite groves. The Fairbank Historic Townsite is open daily for self-guided tours. Trails lead to the river and a hilltop cemetery. The schoolhouse, serving as museum and visitor center, is open Friday through Sunday, manned by knowledgeable volunteers from Friends of the San Pedro River. Fairbank sits along Arizona 82, southwest of Kartchner Caverns.

Lost Dutchman State Park

Nearest Town: Apache Junction.

Why Go: Known for spring wildflower displays and gorgeous hiking trails, the park stretches across cactus-strewn flats to the edge of the Superstition Mountains, a towering wall of volcanic cliffs rising from the desert floor.

This is a land of legends and ghosts, of murdered men and hidden gold.

Named for a fabled gold mine, Lost Dutchman State Park laps at the base of the Superstition Mountains, a sudden and savage precipice, a barrier of sheer dark stone. This is where civilization ends and wilderness begins.

Somewhere deep within that sun-blasted maze of volcano bones lies a secret gold mine overflowing with riches. Or maybe it's just a pilfered cache of gold nuggets. Or maybe there's nothing but rock and cacti and coyote droppings as far as the eye can see. It all depends whom you ask.

Did the Dutchman discover gold in the Superstition Mountains? Geologists say no. Treasure hunters say absolutely and they have the map to prove it. What we do know for sure is that there was no Dutchman. Never was.

Jacob Waltz was German.

Gold Fever

There are several variations of the tale of the Lost Dutchman Mine, but the main thrust goes like this: During the 1840s the Peralta family of Mexico operated several mining claims, one of them a rich gold mine in the Superstitions. An expedition returning gold ore to Mexico was attacked by Apaches and all the miners perished except one, or maybe two.

Although many searched for the missing

Brittlebush blooms along the trails at Lost Dutchman State Park. Photo by the author.

mine, it was German-born Jacob Waltz who made the big find in the 1870s, possibly aided by information from a member of the Peralta family. Waltz worked the mine and allegedly killed anyone, including his former partner, who came too close to his discovery. He never displayed more than a small stash of gold.

On his deathbed in 1891, Waltz finally described the location of the mine to Julia Thomas, a neighbor that had been caring for him. Neither she nor any of the hundreds of treasure seekers have ever found the storied hole. Gruesome murders and strange disappearances followed, cementing the sinister reputation of the Superstitions.

Of course, there are some problems with the lurid tale. Geologists contend that no

substantial vein of gold would form in the volcanic fissures of the Superstitions. There's no real evidence that the Peralta massacre ever took place. And owning a fabulous gold mine didn't seem to benefit Waltz. He lived in a modest shack and died nearly penniless. None of this dissuaded those that came seeking untold riches. There is the truth, and there are legends. Then there are rumors of gold, and those outweigh everything.

Fast Fact: One theory of Jacob Waltz's gold is that he stole nuggets from the Vulture Mine near Wickenburg or Goldfield at the edge of the Superstitions and used that bit of color to represent a larger find.

Not Those Kinds of Mountains

If your notion of mountains involves snow-capped peaks, fragrant forests, and sweeping meadows, the Superstitions will slap the wide-eyed innocence right off your face. The Supes, as they're known locally, are towering ramparts of welded tuff, granite, dacite, and basalt. They're part fortress, part maze—the hulking skeletons of ancient volcanoes. They don't need a puny gold mine to make them mysterious.

Some 25 million years ago, a series of volcanoes lashed this region, spewing ash and lava. The volcanoes collapsed into their partly emptied magma chambers, producing depressions or calderas. A subsequent upthrust of thick lava within the largest of these calderas followed. Eons of erosion have gnawed the Superstitions into the fierce range of jagged cliffs and slashing canyons punctuated by curious hoodoos that we see today.

Lost Dutchman State Park makes the perfect base camp to admire or explore this

Fast Fact: The Apache Trail Historic Road is one of Arizona's most scenic drives, traversing a volcanic landscape, skirting a chain of lakes, and plunging precariously down Fish Creek Hill. The former stagecoach route was completed in 1905 to accommodate construction of Roosevelt Dam.

wild landscape. Enter the park off Arizona 88, the famed Apache Trail. A paved road winds through the lower end, connecting campground loops, picnic areas, and trailheads.

The park supports a beautiful network of trails for hikers and bikers, rambling across the front slope below the sheer rocky walls. Some stay within the confines of the park, while others enter the national forest and connect to longer routes that plunge deeper into the Supes. It's easy to put together a perfect outing for all skill levels. And I do mean all.

Sunset colors add a touch of drama to the Superstition Mountains at Lost Dutchman. Courtesy of Arizona State Parks and Trails, Phoenix.

Happy Trails

The Native Plant Trail is a quarter-mile wheelchair-accessible paved path that identifies many of the common plants of the Sonoran Desert. The Discovery Trail connects campground and day-use areas and features informational signs, bird feeders, and a wildlife pond. Treasure Loop makes a moderate 2.4-mile climb to the base of the cliff for a closer view of the craggy rock formations and returns. Jacob's Crosscut slashes across the park, then stretches for an additional 4.5 miles along the base of the mountains. The Prospector's View angles toward the mountains and connects Treasure Loop, Jacob's Crosscut, and Siphon Draw, allowing hikers a variety of options. Along the way enjoy big panoramas of the mountains and the valley below.

The Siphon Draw Trail provides a great introduction to the Superstitions. It launches from the Saguaro day-use area and then turns onto an old wagon road pointed toward the high cliffs. As soon as it exits the park, the trail turns steeper and narrower. It's a straight climb up the gullet of those hardscrabble mountains. Exotic carved rock formations close around you as you climb. The official trail ends in a basin of polished stone. After rains, the water flows down the walls, filling a bowl at one end.

This should be your turnaround spot. A few hardy, or perhaps deranged, souls continue upward from here toward the Flatiron, the big formation that resembles the bow of a ship jutting from the mountainside high above you. But be warned: This is an unmarked, sketchy, and perilous route, considered one of the most difficult trails in the state. It should only be attempted by experienced and well-prepared hikers.

The park also has 4 miles of mountain-bike single track at the base of Superstition Mountain, a winding loop rated beginning to intermediate. Bikers can also continue

Exotic rock formations can be seen from the Siphon Draw Trail. Photo by the author.

on trails that exit the park and cross national-forest land. However, bikes are not permitted to pass the wilderness boundary on the Siphon Draw Trail.

Big Blooming Springs

There is also a softer side of the Supes. Following wet winters, Lost Dutchman State Park can put on one of Arizona's most dramatic wildflower displays. It's an astonishing sight to pull into the park and see the juxtaposition of those ragged volcanic cliffs floating above a sea of Mexican gold poppies. It feels like a scene plucked from *The Wizard of Oz*, except with Gila monsters instead of flying monkeys.

Of course, it all depends on receiving the right amount of rain, and temperatures that aren't too hot. Poppies are delicate little divas and don't handle excessive heat very well. The most vivid shows of color can start in late February and run through April. Even following dry winters, there's usually a nice display of color at Lost Dutchman because of the perennial blooms of chuparosa, globe mallow, and especially the reliable brittlebush. Elbowing aside cactus and stone, defying drought and bug, the sunburst yellow blossoms of brittlebush almost always arrive as scheduled.

Yet the poppies are the showstoppers. Whether they appear in isolated clusters or

drown the hillsides in a crescendo of lumi-
nous orange is the final determining factor
in what separates the unbelievable years
from the simply remarkable.

Yet no matter what the conditions, I
show up to Lost Dutchman every wildflower season, usually more than once.
Growing up in Ohio, I always feuded with
winter, a cantankerous, disagreeable season.
Since moving to Arizona, I've taken great
delight in spending every February day I
can rambling around the desert in shorts
and T-shirt, searching for colorful blooms.
Revenge is a dish best served balmy.

What's the absolute worst thing that can
happen? I hike the trails on the flanks of
the legendary Superstition Mountains on a
satiny soft late-winter day, reveling in gentle sunshine and spectacular views, and I
only get to admire hundreds of flowers
instead of thousands? Boohoo.

When You Go

Lost Dutchman State Park is located in
Apache Junction, 40 miles east of Phoenix.
6109 North Apache Trail, 480-928-4485,
azstateparks.com.

Admission

$ per vehicle (up to four adults).

Cabins

Lost Dutchman features five heated,
air-conditioned cabins with sweet mountain views. Each cabin comes equipped
with a queen bed, two sets of bunk beds, a

table, chairs, and a covered wooden porch.
Bring your own bedding or sleeping bags,
towels, utensils, and so on. And pack a
flashlight for nighttime walks to the
restrooms and showers.

Camping

The campground has 134 sites. Of those, 68
have electric and water, and the remainder
are nonhookup sites, on paved roads, for
tents or RVs. Every site has a picnic table, a
barbecue grill, and a fire pit. There are no
size restrictions on RVs.

Events

Guided hikes, photography workshops,
geology talks, and star parties are offered
on a regular basis during the cooler months
of the year.

Picnic Areas

13 shade ramadas with tables, grills, and
lovely mountain views are found along the
main park road. So even nonhikers can
enjoy the vistas.

Trails

Lost Dutchman features six trails ranging
from easy to strenuous. Some exit the park
and continue across national-forest land.
Some trails are open to mountain biking.
Pick up a trail map upon entry and inquire
about suitable trails for your experience
level. This is desert terrain. Wear a hat, sun-
glasses, and sunscreen, and carry plenty of
water.

Nearby Attractions

The Superstition Mountain Museum
houses an extensive collection that mingles
history, folklore, and Hollywood. Along
with the main building, the grounds
include a rare 20-stamp mill and a well-
drilling machine, in addition to the
Apacheland Barn and Elvis Memorial
Chapel, structures that survived a fire at

nearby Apacheland Movie Ranch. Through the years, dozens of movies and television shows were filmed at Apacheland, including *Gunfight at the O.K. Corral, Wanted: Dead or Alive*, and *Charro!*, starring Elvis Presley in a nonsinging role. The museum includes exhibits on Native Americans, wildlife, ranching, and the history of the mountains, and of course displays plenty of maps to the Lost Dutchman Mine. If you're planning on finding the gold, this is a good place to start. 4087 North Apache Trail, 480-983-4888, superstitionmountain museum.org.

Just across the highway from Lost Dutchman State Park is Goldfield Ghost Town. The former mining camp had a short life. A vein of gold was discovered in 1892, but it soon played out. The re-created town features weathered plank buildings, creaky wooden sidewalks, and majestic mountain vistas. Arizona's only narrow-gauge train circles the town. Take a short mine tour, visit a museum and a bordello, and watch gunfights that break out hourly during the busy season. The Goldfield Gunfighters may be no-good varmints but they're punctual no-good varmints. 480-983-0333, goldfieldghosttown.com.

Operating out of Goldfield, Apache Trail Tours is a jeep company that offers off-road adventures and on-road scenic rides. Explore the spectacular and harrowing Apache Trail past a chain of lakes, down steep mountainsides, and around hairpin curves. Or head for the desert outback. Apache Trail Tours is the only company permitted for off-roading in this corner of the national forest. Tackle some rough terrain, visit ancient ruins, and even pan for gold. Knowledgeable guides will keep you entertained and informed. 480-982-7661, www.apachetrailtours.com.

McFarland State Historic Park

Nearest Town: Florence.
Why Go: Visit the oldest standing courthouse in Arizona, one of 120 buildings on the National Register of Historic Places that make up downtown Florence, where exhibits cover everything from Old West gunfights to the large-scale POW camp operated in town during World War II.

If your holiday shopping list fairly bristles with people that are hard to buy for, plan a trip to McFarland Courthouse. The small gift shop there is filled with an assortment of items you won't find anywhere else. Imagine the smiles on Christmas morning from even the most persnickety recipient when they unwrap a birdhouse built from license plates, or a license-plate pencil holder. Especially when you explain that they weren't made by Santa's elves but by inmates at Florence State Prison.

When the prison gift shop closed in 2014, inmates needed a new outlet for their creative endeavors and found it, ironically enough, at the former courthouse. There are other metal artworks, wind chimes, shot glasses, and coffee mugs adorned with a drawing of the prison and the words "Gated Community" or "Florence Bed and Breakfast." You have to admire convicts that can maintain a wry sense of humor.

And if you like to set out a plate of cookies for Santa, you can get them from the same boys and girls that may be on the Naughty list. Cookies, tortillas, and a light wheat bread that's high in fiber are all baked by inmates and delivered to the gift

Fast Fact: The Arizona Prison at Florence opened in 1908, built by inmates. It replaced the Yuma Territorial Prison.

The adobe brick building known as McFarland Courthouse was completed in 1878. Photo by the author.

shop each Friday. Be sure to place your order by Wednesday.

McFarland State Historic Park is located in downtown Florence. It consists of a preserved courthouse and other buildings dating to the Arizona Territory period.

Sweet Home Adobe

Florence was founded in 1866, making it one of Arizona's oldest non–Native American settlements. They've done a remarkable job of preserving a past that's both bloody and pastoral. Sitting on the banks of the Gila River, Florence began as a farming community that boomed in 1875 when silver was discovered in nearby mountains.

Downtown Florence retains that Western character with more than 120 buildings listed on the National Register of Historic Places. Many of the structures date back to the 1870s and '80s, and range from Sonoran style to Arizona Territorial, American Victorian, and Mission Revival.

The courthouse, the first in Pinal County, was built in 1878 of adobe bricks. Lumber for the roof and floors was hauled by wagon from the forests of northern Arizona. Courtroom, judge's chambers, sheriff's office, and jail occupied the first floor. The second story was used as a jury room and quarters for visiting lawmen. In less troublesome times, the courthouse was also the site of dances and social gatherings.

It's the oldest standing courthouse in Arizona and the largest adobe structure from the territorial period.

Although not as famous as its Tombstone counterpart, the Pinal County Courthouse saw its share of violence and then some. In 1883 local vigilantes stormed the sheriff's office, dragged two prisoners from their cells, and hanged them in the corridor of the jail. The men had been charged with robbing the stage and killing the guard. Members of the mob were never brought to justice.

They must have been a rowdy, impatient bunch in Florence because soon after the first necktie party, they tried to lynch other prisoners. This time the jailer hustled the prisoners up to the second floor and armed them. The crowd suddenly lost interest.

Big Mac

When a larger courthouse was built in 1891, the adobe building became the county hospital. It later served as a museum. In 1974 former governor Ernest W. "Mac" McFarland purchased the building and donated it to Arizona State Parks.

McFarland first arrived in Phoenix in 1919. While serving in the US Navy during World War I, he contracted a bronchial infection and nearly died. Following surgery, he was discharged and sought out a drier climate. He went on to an unparalleled career as a public servant. McFarland is the only person in Arizona's history to serve in the top three positions in state government—as a United States senator (including being majority leader from 1951 to 1953), as a governor, and as Chief Justice of the Arizona Supreme Court.

Known as the "Father of the GI Bill," McFarland was also instrumental in the formation of the Central Arizona Project, acquiring water from the Colorado River. While governor, he signed Arizona State Parks into being in 1957. The courthouse was named to honor the statesman, who passed away in 1984.

Following the budget cutbacks of 2009, McFarland State Historic Park was closed for two years. Arizona State Parks forged a partnership with the town of Florence and the Main Street Program, which now manages the facility. The old adobe courthouse also serves as the Florence Visitor Center.

The building has been restored and stocked with period furniture in the offices and courtroom. Numerous exhibits reflect the history of the building and community. One cabinet contains medical equipment and supplies from the nearly 50 years it

The first courthouse built in Pinal County also served as a hospital before becoming a state park. Photo by the author.

served as the town hospital. An archives building houses the McFarland papers. A collection of photographs, journals, maps, and artifacts pertains to the Florence prisoner-of-war camp. The facility was Arizona's largest POW camp, holding over 13,000 German and Italian prisoners during World War II.

Shootout at the Tunnel Saloon

One display at the courthouse tells a story in simple terms. It's just a mirror sporting an angry bullet hole. The mirror comes from the Tunnel Saloon, site of one of the Old West's classic gunfights.

As Pinal County Sherriff, Pete Gabriel hired Joe Phy as deputy. Phy was also an experienced lawman but was eventually fired by Gabriel over misconduct. As a result, Phy's hatred for his former friend and boss seethed. The bad blood brewing came to a head on a May evening in 1888.

By then, Gabriel had retired as sheriff, tried his hand at mining, and come up short. He had returned to Florence and was drinking in the Tunnel Saloon when Phy burst in. Heated words were exchanged and both men slapped leather. All told, 11 shots were fired. Gabriel was hit in the chest and the groin, and Phy soaked up lead like a sponge. Mortally wounded, Phy staggered outside to the sidewalk. Gabriel followed, stepping over his one-time deputy, and stumbled down the street before collapsing.

Phy bled out a few hours later. Although told his wounds were fatal, Gabriel survived. He lived another 10 years, but it was said the killing of Phy forever haunted him.

A Slice of Americana

Walk outside the courthouse and it feels like a step back in time. The entire downtown is registered as a National Historic District. Before leaving the visitor center, grab a map for details of the official walking tour.

Throughout downtown old adobes are interspersed with elegant Victorians, Mission Revival styles, cozy bungalows, and early twentieth-century commercial structures, including the coolest hardware store in the state. It's the kind of place where you expect to find Mark Twain shopping for roofing nails, being waited on by Elvis.

To go along with the stamped-tin ceiling, wooden floors, and aisles crowded with goods, there's a welcome hominess

Fast Fact: Charles Poston led the fight to have Arizona granted territorial status in 1863 and was declared the "Father of Arizona." He served as the territory's first delegate to Congress and is entombed near Florence atop Poston Butte.

everyone should experience. Grab a free bag of popcorn and browse around. The friendly staff won't mind. Along with the essentials, there are knickknacks, candy, hats, gifts, décor items, and even a talking prospector mannequin. It always reminds me of the old-fashioned general store that used to anchor every downtown. It's nice to know a few are still hanging in there.

When You Go

McFarland State Historic Park is located at 24 West Ruggles Street, 520-868-5216, azstateparks.com. Both the park and visitor center are open from 9:00 a.m. to 5:00 p.m. Monday through Saturday, October

Pearl Hart made a name for herself when she pulled one of the very last stagecoach robberies. In 1899 Hart, while dressed in men's clothing, and her accomplice, Joe Boot, held up the stage that ran between Globe and Florence. They relieved the passengers of more than $400 and a couple of pistols. Hart did hand back each a dollar so they'd have eating money when they arrived in Florence.

A sheriff's posse quickly scooped up the outlaws. Hart was sent to a Tucson jail because Florence had no facilities for women. There she promptly escaped (with the help of an enamored accomplice), but was arrested two weeks later. Hart and Boot were convicted—5 years for her, 30 for him—and sent to Yuma Territorial Prison. Neither served out their terms.

Boot was made a trusty and simply walked away while outside the walls and was never heard of again. Hart, who had garnered nationwide headlines, charmed her way into a private mountainside cell and yard. Then she was abruptly pardoned in 1902. It's rumored that she became pregnant while in the slammer, which could have been an embarrassing revelation for officials.

After her release, Hart had a brief show-business career and then largely disappeared from public view. It's believed she married an Arizona rancher and lived out her days quietly not far from the scene of her crime.

through May. They close at 2:00 p.m. June through September.

Admission

Free.

Events

AROUND TOWN

With so many vintage structures, the Florence Historic Home Tour is always eagerly anticipated. Every February, visitors explore several beautifully restored buildings and get a closer look at the architectural flourishes that make Florence such a surprising gem.

Picnic Areas

There are three picnic tables and a grill located under shade trees in the courtyard.

Nearby Attractions

The Tom Mix Memorial is located a few miles south of Florence on Arizona 79. It's a quiet place in the desert with shaded picnic tables overlooking a forest of creosote bushes, chain-fruit chollas, and saguaros. On an October afternoon in 1940, the "King of the Cowboys" was killed when he lost control of his speeding Cord Phaeton convertible and rolled into a dry wash. Mix made 291 Westerns, most of them silent, and defined the role of the white-hatted hero saving the day. He was also a rodeo star, circus performer, and a pallbearer at Wyatt Earp's funeral. A plaque and a statue of a saddled horse with bowed head mark the spot where the old cowboy made his last ride.

An impressive four-story structure rises in Coolidge just west of Florence, made of earth and still standing after 700 years. Casa Grande Ruins National Monument protects the largest single building left from Hohokam culture. Standing 35 feet tall, Casa Grande, or Big House, was built of unreinforced clay (caliche) in the mid-1300s and is believed to have been used for astronomical observation. Also on the grounds are an excellent museum, smaller structures, and a ceremonial ball court. 520-723-3172, www.nps.gov/cagr.

The Pinal County Historical Society Museum located in downtown Florence is a delicious combination of frivolity and the macabre, just like all museums should be. Visitors can wander past a room of lovely cactus furniture built in the 1930s to a display of nooses used in hangings, with corresponding mug shots of the prisoners who left this earth wearing them. In between is a nice mix of exhibits that range from a Civil War spy story to a blacksmith shop to cowboy memorabilia, including a Tom Mix collection. They close from mid-July through the end of August for a summer break. 715 South Main Street, 520-868-4382, www.pinalcountyhistoricalmuseum.org.

Oracle State Park

Nearest Town: Oracle.
Why Go: This 4,000-acre wildlife refuge in the foothills of the Santa Catalina Mountains, a hiking and biking paradise, shelters a portion of the Arizona Trail as well as the historic and unique Mediterranean-style Kannally Ranch House.

Oracle came all the way back from the dead. No other park suffered as Oracle did during the bloodletting of 2009. Oracle was one of a handful of parks that shut down completely. And it stayed closed long after the others had bounced back. The park reopened on a limited basis in 2012 but didn't return to a full seven-days-per-week schedule until 2017.

That's hard to understand because this place, located north of Tucson in the foothills of the Santa Catalina Mountains, is full of surprises. It offers two very distinctive experiences to a couple of audiences. First, it is a hiker and biker haven with over 15 miles of trails weaving among its varying habitats of oak woodland and desert scrub. Most notably it is the only state park that contains a piece of that epic route, the Arizona Trail. Stretching from the Mexican border all the way to Utah, the Arizona National Scenic Trail covers 800 miles of wildly diverse terrain—and 4 of those miles cross the rolling hills of Oracle State Park.

Yet the centerpiece of the park has nothing whatsoever to do with people in scuffed hiking boots and sweat-streaked T-shirts. It is an exquisite home of white stucco and turquoise wood shutters, built into a hillside. The Kannally Ranch House is of Mediterranean Revival style with Moorish influences patterned on Italianate villas of the 1920s.

Not the sort of place you expect to find in the middle of cattle country just down the road from Buffalo Bill's mine.

Go West, Young Man

Back in the day, men streamed west to the Arizona Territory for a variety of reasons, but primarily they came in search of wealth or health. For Neil Kannally it was the latter. Neil left his Illinois home in 1902 seeking sunshine and a dry climate. He settled at a tuberculosis health resort in Oracle.

As he grew stronger, Neil's brother Lee arrived, and the two men purchased a 160-acre ranch dating back to the 1880s. More siblings soon arrived—Molly, Vincent, and the youngest, 7-year-old Lucile. The cattle business was good and the ranch continued to expand until it covered 50,000 acres. By now the old adobe homestead must have

The Kannally Ranch House is at the heart of the Oracle State Park story. Courtesy of Rick Mortensen, Cincinnati.

felt pretty crowded, so the boys built another cottage for their two sisters.

In 1929 the Kannallys began construction on the ranch house we know today. Over 2,600 square feet of space is spread across four levels. The walls are double adobe, 18 inches thick. The house contains three spiral staircases, including one of natural stone. Slate floor tiles were cut in Vermont. Towering windows overlook a European-style garden and the rolling ranchland. Designed by architect H. Newkirk, construction was completed in 1932.

The grand home had everything: modern kitchen, formal dining room, great room, solarium, and servant's apartment—only bedrooms were missing. For as long as they lived in the house, the family would retire at night by climbing down the hill on the narrow stone staircase to the original ranch adobe and the sisters' cottage.

In the 1950s, with the boys getting older, the family sold off the mineral rights and all but 4,000 acres of the land to the Magma Copper Company.

None of the siblings ever married. The last surviving Kannally was Lucile who died in 1976. Before passing, she deeded the home and 4,000 acres to the Defenders of Wildlife. A decade later, they turned the property over to Arizona State Parks.

Home Sweet Home

Today, the Kannally Ranch House has been beautifully restored thanks to the park and to hard-working volunteers. The Friends of Oracle State Park raise funds and donate their time to repair and maintain the ranch house—which is on the National Register of Historic Places—and its grounds.

Most of the original features are still intact, and many of the original pieces of furniture give the place that homey feel, such as the Kannally dining-room table, which was often expanded to welcome guests. Lucy loved to entertain.

Adorning the walls of the living room are nearly 30 Impressionist-style paintings with a Western flavor. The colorful oils are the work of Lee Kannally, who suffered nerve-gas poisoning in World War I and developed tremors. He took up painting as a form of therapy. Lee would lay the canvas on the ground and lean forward to paint.

Ranger-led tours of Kannally Ranch House are offered Saturday and Sunday at 11 a.m. No reservation is needed. The tour is free with park admission. Of course, visitors are welcome to explore the gracious home on their own whenever the park is open, which thankfully is now every darn day.

On the Trail

While I love a home tour as much as anybody, all those trails were calling to me.

The park offers a series of interconnected trails, so it's easy to put together outings suitable for all ages and abilities. The 1.2-mile Nature Trail Loop makes a good introduction as it traverses scrubby hills affording views of the Galiuro Mountains and the San Pedro River Valley. During wet springs this is one of the best flower shows in the park. The trail also passes a wildlife blind in Cottonwood Wash. This is where a mountain lion is regularly photographed. Now it feels like a trail, right?

My favorite hike is probably Granite Overlook Loop, 1.6 miles total. It circles through hills that are dotted with clusters of boulders. Oak and mesquite trees rise from a sea of tall grass. Stalks of yuccas and bear grass wave at each other from ridgeline to ridgeline.

Take the trail counterclockwise. That way you'll make a short but steep climb and have a long, gradual descent. Steep downhills with this surface of crushed granite pebbles can make for tricky footing. The trail crosses the park's highest point (4,622 feet) and offers impressive views of the

Oracle is the only state park that includes a segment of the Arizona National Scenic Trail. Photo by the author.

ranch house shimmering white in the Arizona sun.

Naturally, being so close, I couldn't resist taking a bite out of the Arizona Trail. I hoofed out on the Wildlife Corridor Trail and after 1.6 miles junctioned with the Big Kahuna. A left turn would take me to Utah. Hang a right and I could mosey down Old Mexico way.

Both options sounded good, but since I was low on water I stayed in the park. I turned right and ambled for a couple of miles on the Arizona National Scenic Trail, then returned via the Manzanita Trail for a 6-mile outing.

I enjoyed an especially nice moment on the last leg of the hike. The Manzanita dips in and out of some washes and the vegetation gets a bit heavier closer to the parking lot. Oracle State Park is a wildlife refuge teeming with a roster of animals that includes white-tailed deer, javelinas, coyote, fox, all four Arizona skunks, bobcats, and the occasional mountain lion. But so far I hadn't seen many critters, which was not surprising on a warm midday hike.

In the last quarter mile I startled a couple of deer that went bounding off through the oaks. Then just a little further on, I happened to glance to my left and there was another one, a doe no more than 30 yards away. But instead of making a hurried exit, she stood motionless, in perfect profile but with her face turned toward me.

We were both in the open and we stood without moving for what seemed like several long minutes. She looked perfectly at ease, a very calm presence, more curious than nervous. Her eyes redefined the concept of brown. I was going to have to rethink everything I knew about the color.

Birds sang in the oak branches. A faint

breeze rustled the leaves. The afternoon sun streaked the grass with golden highlights. There seemed to be plenty of time to study all the details as we pondered each other.

I slowly moved a hand toward my camera and the spell was broken. With a jump she vanished in the brush. I should have known better. I'm no tourist. This was strictly a trail moment. It couldn't exist on film or anywhere else.

Hikers will understand. I spend time on the trail collecting as many of those personal and perfect diamond-shaped moments as I can. Fleeting though they may be in real time, they last for years in memory.

That's what hiking is all about.

When You Go

Oracle State Park is located in the town of Oracle off Arizona 77, approximately 35 miles north of Tucson. The park is open from 7:00 a.m. to 5:00 p.m. The American Avenue–trailhead parking lot (just outside the park) is always open to accommodate after-hours use by hikers of the Arizona Trail and stargazers. 520-896-2425, azstateparks.com.

Admission

$ per vehicle (for up to four adults).

Dark Skies

In 2014 Oracle State Park was designated as an International Dark Sky Park. This prestigious designation recognizes the park as an exceptional place to view the wonders of the night sky. Oracle is far enough away from most light-pollution sources, making the Milky Way visible along with many other celestial objects. Visitors can access the American Avenue parking area seven days a week. This lot is open for viewing the night sky or for access to the Arizona National Scenic Trail as well.

Events

Ranger-led tours of Kannally Ranch House are offered Saturday and Sunday at 11:00 a.m. No reservation is needed. The tour is free with park admission.

Guided bird and nature walks and full-moon hikes are occasionally scheduled. Stargazing events with telescope viewing, and events that include guest speakers and live music, are regular occurrences. Check the website for specific dates.

Picnic Areas

There are tables on the gracious patio of the Kannally Ranch House. Additional picnic tables can be found under shade trees at the Oak Woodland Area.

School Groups

Environmental Education Field Trip Programs for school groups are scheduled on weekdays. These programs are conducted along trails so that students can learn about habitat and the interrelationships between plants, animals, and people. Make reservations by calling the park office.

Trails

The park contains over 15 miles of hiking trails for use by hikers, mountain bikers, and equestrians. In addition, a section of the Arizona National Scenic Trail crosses through the park. Here are several other trails:

Bellota Trail (0.8-mile loop) and *Windy Ridge Trail* (1-mile loop) are both used for environmental-education school programs and are open only to hikers. No dogs are permitted.

Mariposa Trail (1.2 miles) connects the park road to the American Avenue parking lot. It's named for the colorful mariposa lilies that bloom in spring.

Powerline Trail leaves from the American Avenue lot and follows a ridge northeast before cutting back through the park, crossing Cherry Valley Wash and joining the Arizona Trail for a stretch. It finally ends at wide Cottonwood Wash, which will lead back to the Kannally House. Look for an old homestead site near a ridgeline on the *Windmill Loop Trail* (4.1 miles), which connects part of the Arizona Trail with the Powerline Trail.

Nearby Attractions

The Acadia Ranch Museum is housed in the original 1880s ranch headquarters, saved from ruin and restored by the Oracle Historical Society. It showcases the area's past with exhibits on ranching and mining. There are several photos of Buffalo Bill in Oracle, and there is a charming photo collection of old-time picnics among distinctive rock formations. The Tuberculosis Room displays medical antiques and artifacts from the days when the Acadia Ranch was a health resort for "lungers." Hours are limited. 825 East Mount Lemmon Highway, 520-896-9609, www.oracle historicalsociety.org.

Biosphere 2 rises like a futuristic greenhouse a few miles south of Oracle. This giant experiment houses seven model ecosystems, earning it the title of the world's largest earth-science lab. The facility is run by the University of Arizona for research purposes, but tours are also available. Visitors can wander through a tropical rainforest and savanna grasslands and can even smell an ocean complete with coral reef. 520-621-4800, biosphere2.org.

Arizona Zipline Adventures offers the state's longest zipline eco-tour, soaring over the landscape at speeds of up to 60 mph. The course consists of five lines that vary in length from 400 feet to 1,500 feet. Located just outside of Oracle, Peppersauce Station (your starting point) includes a store and restaurant. Reservations are required for tours. Sunset and moonlight tours are also available. 520-308-9350, www.ziparizona. com.

Patagonia Lake State Park and Sonoita Creek State Natural Area

Nearest Town: Patagonia.
Why Go: A beloved lake hidden among rolling hills borders an unspoiled riparian area offering hiking trails and backcountry campsites.

Water is a precious resource in a desert state. So it should come as no surprise that we keep much of ours hidden for safekeeping. It's not always easy to find. Often our riverbeds are full of gravel, boulders, cacti, and trees—everything but good old H2O, which makes only an occasional appearance following snowmelt or angry storms.

Lakes can be just as elusive. They often fill canyons or narrow valleys. Anywhere that forms a suitable catch basin will do. Most lakes in Arizona are man-made but that doesn't mean we love them any less than the natural ones.

A Hidden Lake

Patagonia Lake is like that. It's a long, slender waterway, almost fiord-like, that's tucked away amid the slanted hills and golden grasslands of southern Arizona. When you make the turn off the highway south of Patagonia and follow the signs toward a lake, it seems like someone's idea of a joke.

The slopes are whiskered with ocotillos, plants with long, spindly branches rising in

Fast Fact: Nestled between the Patagonia and Santa Rita Mountains, the treelined hamlet of Patagonia is known as an arts community and a haven for birders.

Patagonia Lake is one of southern Arizona's hidden gems. Courtesy of Rick Mortensen, Cincinnati.

a cluster. To conserve water, ocotillos only leaf out after being prompted by a serious rain. They shed their small leaves as soon as dry conditions return, which means they spend much of their lives stark naked. When the wind blows, their branches rattle like a skeleton orgy.

When you have a dense grove of ocotillos with lifeless-looking branches, it can be eerie. So the idea that these parched twigs are somehow the gatekeepers to a sprawling lake seems absurd. But just about the time you're ready to flip a U-turn, you round a bend and spot a glint of blue winking from down below.

What you'll experience at the lake depends on what time of year you arrive. Patagonia Lake is the seasonal Jekyll and Hyde of state parks. From fall through spring, the campground is filled with birders. Avian-adventure boat tours quietly prowl the lake several times a day. Ranger-led bird walks are regular events. Visitors carry binoculars and cameras with lenses the size of rocket launchers as they tiptoe

Families enjoy some fun on the beach at Patagonia Lake. Photo by the author.

through the cottonwoods and willows along the shoreline.

Then around mid-April, most of the birders move on, the visitor center closes, and the recreationists begin to arrive. Boaters, swimmers, skiers, and water lovers of all sorts, a slightly more boisterous crowd, come to camp or spend a day. For the summer, Patagonia Lake becomes Tucson's unofficial beach.

The 265-acre lake makes a shimmering oasis in the high desert any time of year. A campground clings to the south side of the lake. Cabins were added in 2018. Plus, there are several boat-in campsites available. A wide sandy beach features a roped-off swimming area. Shaded picnic tables sit at the water's edge. A market sells food, drinks, ice, and fishing supplies, and a marina rents boats.

So minutes after you arrive you can be paddling past the cattails into open water. The eastern half of the lake is a no-wake zone, and the western side is more wide open for boaters and skiers. One hiking trail traces the edge of the lake. But if you really want a good stretch of the legs, go next door.

Au Naturel

Adjacent to Patagonia Lake, the Sonoita Creek State Natural Area (SCSNA) offers an entirely different experience. No matter what's going on at the lake, plenty of solitude can be found amid a smorgasbord of habitats. Also administered by the state park system, the natural area protects the Sonoita Creek and Coal Mine Spring watersheds. While Patagonia Lake is for recreation, the natural area is for conservation and has been left very much undisturbed.

SCSNA can only be accessed via the state park. Proceed to the visitor center to get a free hiking permit for the natural area. The first time I showed up to hike, I snagged my permit and drove toward the natural area with no idea what to expect. I realized I had inadvertently given the ranger my cell number as an emergency contact instead of my wife's. Great, I thought. If anything happens, they can leave a message on my voice mail to tell me I'm missing.

Somehow I survived that initial foray, and I keep coming back for more. Only a limited number of hikers are allowed in SCSNA at any time, so you're assured of some backcountry isolation. And I increase the odds of privacy by always showing up on days of blistering heat. So of course

anyone with good sense is relaxing at the lake. It sounds inviting, but one doesn't become a desert rat due to an abundance of common sense.

Over 20 miles of trails amble from desert grasslands through lush streamside forests and lead to three backcountry campsites for backpackers in Sonoita Creek State Natural Area. I recommend making a couple of short hikes to sample the spectrum. If you like what you see, you can always come back for more.

It's a short drive to the single parking lot at SCSNA. Immediately the Overlook Trail branches off to scramble 500 feet up the grassy slope of a rounded hill. At the top there's a shaded bench where you can catch your breath and savor expansive views of Patagonia Lake, the riparian thread of the creek snaking across open desert, and the dam and spillway. Take note because they'll be part of the next hike. Overlook is a 1.4-mile round trip.

When you're back on level ground, continue on the Sonoita Creek Trail through a dense grove of ocotillos. This is the gateway trail providing access to the other routes deeper in the natural area. It skirts a rocky canyon before dropping into the creek channel through a forest of mesquites, ashes, and willow trees. Sonoita Creek is a lazy little stream, just a trickle with dreams for much of the year. But even good intentions are enough to create a sweet riparian corridor in this arid land.

You can cross the creek to continue on to other trails. But be alert. Cattle in the area create their own pathways to and from the water, and it's easy to go astray. But I usually just turn onto the signed Blackhawk Canyon Trail and begin making my way back. The two trails form a loop that's about 3 miles.

Blackhawk follows the creek for a ways, then climbs a ridge thick with mesquites and ocotillos. There are good views of the

The Overlook Trail in Sonoita Creek State Natural Area provides an expansive view of the lake. Photo by the author.

Fast Fact: Over 130 butterfly species have been reported in the Sonoita Creek / Patagonia Lake area.

rocky canyon carved by the stream, mostly dry at this end. I stopped at a bench with a sign that said simply Jen's Vista. You know there's a story behind that but I've never tried to run it to ground. I like the mystery of it.

It was a lovely perch gazing down at the sharp-cut gorge below. There was a hint of a creek but no flow of water. Then I spotted a small, isolated pool shaded by young willows. The tiny oasis was visible only because I stopped and rested on this quiet bench. This Jen sure knew how to pick her spots.

At the end of the trail, I came to the service road by the spillway. It was a bit of a jolt to see so much water again, but a welcome one. I followed the road, making a

short, steep climb back to the parking lot. Now I was ready to mosey back to the state park. It seemed like a good time to finish the day with a cold beverage while soothing my tired hiker feet in lake water and listening to the sound of music and boats and kids playing on the beach.

When You Go

Patagonia Lake State Park and Sonoita Creek State Natural Area are located 11 miles south of the town of Patagonia on Arizona 82. Gates are closed from 10:00 p.m. to 4:00 a.m. 520-287-6965, azstate parks.com.

Admission

$$ per vehicles (up to four adults).

Boating

Two boat ramps are available at Patagonia Lake. Both motorized and nonmotorized boats are allowed. Personal Water Craft (PWCs), jet skis, water bikes, above-water exhaust boats, and V-8 jet boats are all prohibited.

The lake is divided into two sections. The east end is no-wake speed only, and the west end is for unlimited speed in a counterclockwise direction. High-speed boats can enter the east section but must travel at a no-wake speed.

Water skiing is allowed anytime from October 1 through April 30. From May through September 30, water skiing is only allowed on normal weekdays, no weekends or legal holidays.

Boat rentals are located in the boat-trailer parking lot. Canoes, rowboats, paddle boats, and pontoon boats are available for rent. Call Patagonia Lake Marina at 520-287-2804 for prices.

Cabins

The campground features seven heated, air-conditioned cabins with lake views. Cabins include a queen bed, two sets of bunk beds, a table, chairs, a microwave, a minifridge, and a covered wooden porch. Bring your own bedding or sleeping bags, towels, utensils, and so on. And pack a flashlight for nighttime walks to the restrooms and showers.

Camping

A campground with 105 developed sites sits at the edge of the lake. Each includes a picnic table and fire ring / grill. A dozen boat-in campsites also dot quiet coves, islands, and bits of shoreline. They are accessible only by boat and come with picnic table and fire ring. Some have portable restrooms.

Three backcountry hike-in camping sites are available at Sonoita Creek State Natural Area. The closest one is about 4 miles from the trailhead. Six people maximum per site, and there is a two-night

limit. There are three tent pads and a steel fire ring at each site. Obtain permits at Patagonia Lake.

Events

The Mariachi and Wine Festival at Patagonia Lake State Park occurs in May. Southern Arizona mariachi bands take the stage, putting on a lively, colorful show. Vendors serve up Mexican food, as well as hamburgers, hot dogs, and shaved ice. Plus there's a piñata for the kids. Bring water, lawn chairs, sunscreen, and hats. Local wineries are on hand for tastings.

AROUND TOWN

The Patagonia Fall Festival is a three-day extravaganza of music, food, and art. It's held in October in Patagonia Town Park with a wide range of live music, puppet shows for the kids, demonstration booths, great local food, wine, and more.

Fishing

Largemouth bass, flathead catfish, channel catfish, crappie, bluegill, and sunfish maintain healthy populations in the lake. Rainbow trout are stocked in the winter months only. A valid Arizona fishing license is required for anglers 10 years and older. Fishing licenses can be purchased at the park store.

Park Store

The market is operated by the park concessionaire and is located in the boat-trailer parking lot. They sell fishing licenses, firewood, grocery items, ice cream, soda, beer and wine, and other camping supplies. Contact the market at 520-287-5545.

Swimming

Swimming is permitted anywhere in Patagonia Lake except near the boat launch. There is a roped-off swim area at Boulder Beach, but there is no lifeguard on duty. All parts of the lake are considered to be wild water so swimming is at your own risk.

Trails

Patagonia Lake offers a 0.5-mile trail that leads through a wooded birding area to Sonoita Creek. Over 20 miles of hiking trails cross the Sonoita Creek State Natural Area. Besides those already described, the New Mexico and Arizona Railroad Trail follows the old railroad bed along the stream channel for 5+ miles. The Coal Mine Spring Trail can be combined with a short stretch on the Vista Trail before joining Cat Cave Trail for a 7-mile loop that leads to two of the backcountry campsites. Visitors will be given a map of SCSNA hiking trails when they receive their permit.

Visitor Center

The visitor center is open seasonally. When it is closed, all permits are available at the park-entrance ranger station.

Nearby Attractions

Close to downtown Patagonia, Tucson Audubon's Paton Center for Humming-birds comes with a story. The Paton family began putting out backyard feeders in the 1970s and hummingbirds swarmed the property. Word spread and soon the family began welcoming strangers who came to enjoy the colorful show. After Marion Paton died in 2009, neighbors and friends kept the feeders stocked until the Tucson Audubon Society took over. There are chairs, shade awnings, and a big board listing recent sightings. This small backyard is one of the most reliable places to spot a violet-crowned hummingbird. Free but donations are appreciated. If the gate is open, come on in. 477 Pennsylvania Avenue in Patagonia.

Visit a ghost town, or even spend the night in one. Perched on the eastern flanks of the Santa Rita Mountains, Kentucky Camp served as the headquarters for the Santa Rita Water and Mining Company from 1902 to 1906. The company folded soon after the founder mysteriously plunged to his death from a Tucson hotel window. Five adobes and the ruins of a bar remain. A cabin and headquarters building have been restored by the forest service and can be rented through their Rooms with a View program. The rustic cabin is available for overnight stays. Kentucky Camp is approximately 20 miles north of Patagonia on a dirt road, off of Arizona 83. 520-281-2296, www.fs.usda.gov/coronado.

The Pimeria Alta Museum in Nogales covers the rich history of the lands stretching from northern Sonora to southern Arizona. Early Spanish settlers dubbed the region, home of the Upper Pima Indians, as Pimeria Alta. Housed in the Old City Hall that dates back to 1914, the museum contains artifacts, photographs, jail cells, rotating displays, and three rare murals by bull-fighter and artist Salvador Corona. 136 North Grand Avenue, 520-287-4621, www.pimeriaaltamuseum.org.

Picacho Peak State Park

Nearest Town: Casa Grande.

Why Go: The westernmost battle of the Civil War took place on the flanks of this prominent peak—the same slopes that blaze with spring wildflowers and contain the most challenging hiking trail in the state park system.

On an early March day, I sat on the hard slant of old lava amid a field of shiny, satiny wildflowers. Behind me a jagged spire rose some 1,500 feet above the valley floor. I gazed downslope across the desert scrub. Although there was no way to know, I wondered if poppies grew on the unmarked grave of Lieutenant James Barrett.

On April 15, 1862, the westernmost battle

Picacho Peak serves as a distinctive landmark rising from the desert floor north of Tucson. Courtesy of Arizona State Parks and Trails, Phoenix.

of the Civil War was fought on the rocky flanks of the mountain that's part of an eroded volcanic flow, 40 miles northwest of Tucson. The fierce skirmish involved only two dozen men yet lasted a good part of the afternoon and resulted in a high percentage of casualties—three dead, three wounded, three captured.

It shouldn't have happened at all but young Lieutenant Barrett seemed to have something to prove.

A Many-Faceted Mountain

This is not a big park, covering just over 3,700 acres. Yet within those confines it contains a great network of hiking trails, including the most challenging trail in the state park system. The distinctive peak bears geological and historical significance and often proves to be one of the best spring wildflower spots in Arizona.

Picacho Peak rises in a sudden thrust overlooking Interstate 10 between Casa Grande and Tucson. Visible for miles, the angled pinnacle resembles a jaunty ship slicing through clear desert air. Scattered saguaros march down the slopes.

Arizona is veined with mountain ranges, big and small. Stand-alone peaks are not as common, especially ones as prominent as Picacho. And none come with this type of historic pedigree.

Civil War Spreads West

In February 1862, Captain Sherod Hunter and his Arizona Rangers raised the Confederacy's Stars and Bars above Tucson. The Confederates hoped to expand into the

Fast Fact: The place name is redundant. Picacho means "peak" in Spanish.

Southwest to attain mineral wealth to finance the war effort and gain access to California ports. To counteract this westward incursion, the California Column was formed, consisting of several companies of infantry, cavalry, and artillery.

By early April a portion of California Column, led by Captain William Calloway, had reached an area near present-day Casa Grande. Not knowing how many troops occupied Tucson, he wanted prisoners to interrogate. Calloway sent Lieutenant Barrett with 12 cavalry troopers and a scout around the east side of Picacho, and Lieutenant Ephraim Baldwin with another dozen men to approach from the west. The units were under orders to stay concealed, holding the lower end of the pass as the main column swept down on the Confederate encampment.

Barrett arrived first on the scene and, ignoring orders, led a mounted charge into the rebel camp. Saddles were emptied at the first exchange of gunfire. One Union soldier was killed and four others were wounded, with one dying the next day. Barrett was struck by a bullet in the neck and died instantly. Three of the Confederates were captured. Fierce fighting continued over the next hour. Finally, exhausted and running low on ammunition, the Union cavalry withdrew, allowing the rebels to flee toward Tucson.

Calloway and the column arrived later that afternoon but the damage had been done. There would be no surprise attack on Tucson. He was not kind to the brash lieutenant in his report. According to Calloway, Barrett acting alone rather than in concert "surprised the rebels and should have captured them without firing a shot, if the thing had been conducted properly."

Captain Sherod Hunter and his Rangers left Tucson a month later, just ahead of the advancing Union column. The skirmish at Picacho Pass proved to be the high-water

Fast Fact: While burning piles of hay at Stanwix Station 80 miles east of Fort Yuma, Confederate soldiers exchanged gunfire with Union pickets, wounding one. This encounter marked the westernmost advance of any organized Confederate force during the war.

mark of the Confederacy's westward expansion.

Some years later, United States soldiers returned to search for the men who fell at Picacho Pass. The bodies of the enlisted troopers were removed and buried elsewhere, but the remains of Lieutenant Barrett were never found. He sleeps beneath the poppies to this day.

Golden Hillsides

When conditions are right, the spring wildflower displays are the greatest show in the desert. It all depends on the amount and timing of winter rains, followed by mild temperatures. Years that are too dry or too hot result in spotty, localized color. Perennials like globe mallow, brittlebush, and desert marigold will bloom to some degree every year because they can tolerate the heat and need only enough moisture to produce blooms.

It's the Mexican gold poppies that distinguish the truly unforgettable seasons. These delicate divas are annuals, which means they germinate from seeds. They might lie beneath the soil for years until the right combination of moisture and temperatures triggers their life-force. Then they burst forth, growing an entire lace-leafed little plant that produces beautiful golden flowers. And it all happens in the span of a few weeks.

Some years the poppies might appear in small, isolated clusters. Other times they arrive in force, drenching hillsides in a sea of smiling yellow and orange faces. Picacho

Poppies spill down the slopes at Picacho Peak. Photo by the author.

Peak harbors a seemingly endless supply of poppies. How many show up each spring all depends on circumstances. Wildflower season at Picacho usually starts in mid-February and runs through March.

During good years I make repeated stops at Picacho Peak. I hike on the lower slopes and then find a comfortable spot to relax and pass the time of day with my old friends, the poppies. I love these little free spirits with their smiling upturned faces as if they're catching spilled droplets of sunshine.

The poppies, along with a supporting cast of brittlebushes, globe mallows, desert chicories, lupines, and others, bloom heaviest on the lower flanks of Picacho Peak. They can be enjoyed from roads and picnic areas. Other good sightings can be found on the short, easy Nature Trail, on the stroll to the Children's Cave, and on the moderate Calloway Trail that climbs to an overlook.

Getting to the Top

Naturally, with such a distinctive spire defining the landscape, there will be plenty of people anxious climb it. Keep in mind

---

Fast Fact: A via ferrata (iron road) is a mountain route equipped with steel cables and other fixed anchors.

---

that this is not your typical mountain hike. There are a couple of trails to the summit and both are strenuous and challenging. And here's a weird thing: You're going to need gloves. Picacho Peak is one of the few places in Arizona accessed by *via ferrata*.

The Hunter Trail assails the peak from the north side of the mountain. Launching from Barrett Loop, the 2-mile trail climbs right from the start, moderate at first, then growing more difficult as it heads for a saddle. Soon you're pulling yourself up the sharpest pitches via steel cables. You'll be thankful for the gloves. From the saddle, the trail drops steeply, losing much of that hard-won elevation gain before ascending again. Some final switchbacks and stretches of bare rock adorned with cable lead to the summit.

Sunset Vista Trail (3.1 miles) works its way up the south slope of Picacho. It's a moderate ramble for the first couple of miles, crossing sandy washes and open desert. When it does start to climb, it is steep and unrelenting. It connects to the Hunter Trail and follows the same via ferrata route to the top, where you can enjoy some unobstructed views of southern Arizona.

When You Go

Picacho Peak State Park is located off I-10 on Exit 219, 75 miles south of Phoenix. Gates are closed from 10:00 p.m. to 5:00 a.m. 520-466-3183, azstateparks.com.

Admission

$ per vehicle (up to four adults).

Camping

The campground has 85 electric sites for both tent and RV camping. All sites offer a picnic table and barbecue / fire ring. No water or sewer hookups are available. Generator use is not permitted. There are two handicap-accessible restroom-and-shower buildings.

A strenuous climb takes hikers to the top of Picacho Peak. Courtesy of Arizona State Parks and Trails, Phoenix.

Picnic Areas

Several day-use areas with shaded picnic tables are located at trailheads and along park roads with good views of the peak and the spring wildflowers.

Trails

Hiking to the summit of Picacho Peak via the Hunter Trail and Sunset Vista Trail is difficult. Both trails are steep and exposed. They require navigating sections of bare rock aided by anchored steel cables. Gloves are recommended. Wear sturdy hiking shoes and carry plenty of water. Do not attempt in hot weather.

Calloway Trail is a moderate 0.7-mile climb to an overlook on the shoulder of the peak.

Nature Trail is an easy 0.5-mile loop that includes interpretive signs.

Children's Cave Trail is a 0.2-mile stroll to a shallow cave with kid-friendly signage along the way.

A Civil War Trail was added to the park in 2016. This short ADA trail loops past informational signage and maps that help tell the larger story of the Civil War in Arizona. There's also a stone memorial that was erected for Lieutenant James Barrett in

1928 near the present-day railroad tracks and later moved inside the park.

Nearby Attractions

Just a mile south of the park, Rooster Cogburn Ostrich Ranch is the Disneyland of petting zoos. While the gangly namesake ostriches are definite hits, they've got a great supporting cast of donkeys, goats, ducks, deer, lorikeets, and even stingrays all happy to be fed in a variety of ways. Seconds after you show up with a cup of nectar, you'll be covered with thirsty lorikeets (technicolor miniparrots) that plop down on your arms, hands, and lap. They offer monster-truck tours of the ranch on weekends. A great stop for kids. 520-466-3658, www.roostercogburn.com.

With Eloy boasting the largest drop zone in the world, it's no surprise that skydivers often outnumber birds. But just because someone hesitates to jump from a plane doesn't mean they don't yearn for a jolt of adrenaline. SkyVenture Arizona solves that quandary with a state-of-the-art skydiving wind tunnel. Receive a flight training course, all necessary gear, and flights in the vertical wind tunnel accompanied by an instructor. Eloy is a few miles north of Picacho Peak State Park. 520-466-4640, www.skyventureaz.com.

Roper Lake State Park and Dankworth Pond State Park

Nearest Town: Safford.

Why Go: Picturesque lakes nestled at the base of Mount Graham include amenities such as comfortable cabins, shady play areas, and a natural spring-fed hot tub.

If Roper Lake had more hiking options, you wouldn't be able to keep me away. Lord knows it has everything else—a beautiful lake, panoramas of mighty mountains, shady picnic areas, comfortable cabins, and even a natural hot tub.

For sheer relaxation purposes, Roper Lake is tops in the state park system. Even if you're antsy like me, this is an ideal base camp for a wide range of recreational activities.

Three little burgs—Pima, Thatcher, and Safford—lull you with their quaintness. They're strung shoulder to shoulder along US 70, nestled in a valley of fertile farmland, bookended by two fierce mountain ranges. I'm always smitten by the bucolic setting. Family farms, small ranches, and lovely homes line the streets. These feel like throwback communities. The whole scene is a return to an era of fresh-painted houses, neatly trimmed yards, and neighborly neighbors. It's one barefoot kid with a

fishing pole shy of being a Norman Rockwell painting.

But that sleepy innocence is also a ruse. These folks are sitting on a gold mine of outdoor fun. Gila Box Riparian National Conservation Area, Aravaipa Canyon (a deep, stream-carved wilderness gorge), Black Hills Country Byway (a 21-mile-long rugged drive into the outback), Hot Well Dunes Recreation Area (2,000 acres of rolling sand dunes), and dramatic Swift Trail (a winding scenic drive up the flanks of towering Mount Graham) are just a few of the nearby attractions. And Roper Lake and sister unit Dankworth Pond serve as their own private fishing and swimming holes.

Twilight falls on Roper Lake. Photo by the author.

On the Waterfront

With cabins and a natural stone hot tub, Roper Lake is perfect for folks who like to rough it in style. It's like a state park for high rollers.

The cabins, campgrounds, and picnic areas surround the 30-acre lake. One of the most popular spots is the Island Day Use Area, usually just called the Island. It should be called the Peninsula to be more accurate, but I suppose that lacks a certain exotic romance. A thumb of land pokes into the lake and makes an inviting oasis with a soft lawn of grass, shade trees, picnic tables, and a small slope of beach.

This is an idyllic, family-friendly place seemingly designed with kids in mind. Splash in the water, play in the sand, run barefoot in the grass, and picnic like there's no tomorrow.

Roper Lake contains largemouth bass, crappie, bluegill, sunfish, catfish, and rainbow trout that are stocked in winter months. Boats are limited to small electric motors, helping preserve the backcountry peace and quiet. There are fishing docks and a boat ramp.

The park has three campgrounds. Some sites are suited for tent camping, some for RVs. Although the heat dissuades many from camping in the summer, it doesn't have to be that way.

The Gila Campground includes a handful of rustic cabins near the water's edge. The cabins are simple but are outfitted with electricity and air conditioning / heating. Beds have mattresses but you'll need to bring your own sleeping bag or linen. A porch swing, picnic table, cold-water sink, and fire ring provide for all your other relaxation needs. Restrooms and showers are just a short walk away.

Speaking of short walks, that's about all you'll find at Roper Lake. Officially, the park has 5 miles of trails but most of those are pathways connecting the campgrounds

and day-use areas. There is the Mariah Mesa Trail, a 0.75-mile loop that climbs a creosote-dotted hill offering good views of the Pinaleno Mountains and the surrounding farmland before ending at the hot tub.

Ah, the hot tub. It's one of those unexpected delights to find at a park. The rock-lined pool is fed by a natural artesian hot spring that keeps the water temperature at about 100 degrees year-round. But remember, this is a family spot, so behave appropriately, which translates to keep your drawers on.

Little Sister

If you want to get a bit of a workout before your soak, head for Roper Lake's sister unit, Dankworth Pond. Located about 3 miles south of Roper, Dankworth Pond contains 15 acres of water that was originally used for commercial catfish farming. Today, it holds the same variety of fish as Roper Lake. There's a fishing dock, and visitors can kayak or go out in small boats—but be advised, there is no ramp.

The pond isn't the only attraction in the park. The Dos Arroyos Trail swings through the desert scrub and climbs a low mesa that's the site of a re-created Indian village. The village contains replicas of dwellings, grinding stones, roasting pits, tools, and artifacts accompanied by some informational signage. The area is often used to educate local school groups about Native American history and culture.

The trail continues through a riparian area and returns to Dankworth Pond for a 1.75-mile loop. So you get to stretch your legs, and maybe learn something about the first people to occupy these lands, and when you end up on the backside of the pond, you're treated to some really sweet views of the Pinalenos framed by water and cottonwood trees.

Dankworth Pond is day use only. No camping is allowed. The park does include

Scenic Dankworth Pond should be included in any visit to Roper Lake.
Photo by the author.

Fast Fact: The Pinaleno Mountains have over 7,000 feet of vertical relief, more than any other range in the state. They're anchored by Mount Graham, at 10,720 feet.

picnic ramadas, a playground, and a small wading pool fed by an artesian hot spring. It's one of many hot springs found in Graham County.

When I got back to Roper from Dankworth, a sociable little crowd was gathered at the hot tub, so instead I headed out to the eastern end of the lake. It seemed like a good spot to watch the sun slip beyond the grasp of the Pinalenos and to see the shimmering reflection of a fast-falling dusk in the lake.

Roper is a peaceful lake that always steals my heart a little. I think it's just a desert rat's fascination. To see water in the desert is to witness a miracle. It is a mirage sprung to life. Here is a thing that should not be, yet is. It restores my faith. Anything seems possible because I have found water in the desert.

Turned out to be a nice sunset. Not an over-the-top, lavish production as is often the case, especially during summer monsoons. There weren't enough clouds for that kind of show. But a beautiful swath of gold polished the horizon as the sun dropped behind palm trees down at the other end of the lake. For a moment, the water seemed poised to go up in flames as fingers of reds and golds stretched across the surface. Somewhere a fish did a somersault and I heard his happy splash. A duck flew overhead and the stillness was so complete I listened to his feathers rippling in the wind for a long time after.

Then I was ready for a soak in the hot tub!

When You Go

Roper Lake State Park is located 6 miles south of Safford on US 191. For Dankworth Pond, continue south on 191 for an additional 3 miles. Park hours are from 6:00 a.m. to 10:00 p.m. The entrance gate is closed after hours. 928-428-6760, azstate parks.com.

Admission

$$ per vehicle (up to four adults) allows access to both Roper Lake and Dankworth Pond.

Boating

Roper Lake has one boat ramp located on the east side of the lake. No gas-powered motors are permitted on the lake. The park does not rent watercraft. Kayaks and small boats are permitted at Dankworth Pond, but there is no ramp.

Cabins

Bring your own bedding or sleeping bags, towels, utensils, and so on. And pack a flashlight for nighttime walks to the restrooms and showers.

Camping

There are 50 sites spread across three campgrounds, as well as one 14-site group area. Most have water and electric hookups. Many will accommodate a vehicle of up to 45 feet.

Events

AROUND TOWN

Salsa Fest takes place every September in Safford and celebrates all things salsa. The event features salsa contests, salsa music and dancing, jalapeno- and salsa-eating contests, a car show, a beer garden, and more.

Fishing

Both Roper Lake and Dankworth Pond contain largemouth bass, crappie, bluegill, sunfish, and catfish. Rainbow trout are stocked in winter months. A valid Arizona fishing license is required for anglers 10 years and older. Fishing is not allowed in the swimming area at Roper Lake.

Picnic Areas

Besides the Island, there are several other lakeside picnic-table areas and group ramadas. Most of these include BBQ grills. Glass containers are prohibited on the Island.

Swimming

A designated swimming area with a sandy beach is on the west side of the Island in Roper Lake. In all situations, exercise caution. There is no lifeguard on duty, so swimming is at your own risk. Swimming is not permitted outside the designated area. There is no swimming allowed in Dankworth Pond.

Nearby Attractions

The Gila Box Riparian National Conservation Area protects a rare desert oasis carved by a series of four perennial waterways—the Gila and the San Francisco Rivers, and Bonita and Eagle Creeks. Located 20 miles northeast of Safford, the BLM-managed area covers 23,000 acres of rugged terrain. Visitors will find historic homesteads, cliff dwellings, and plenty of wildlife to go along with two developed campgrounds, picnic areas, hiking trails, and miles of maintained and primitive roads. This is isolated country, so do your research before venturing out. 928-348-4400, www.blm.gov/arizona.

Some trails work out your taste buds more than your knees. This area is the spicy heart of the Salsa Trail, a collection of mom-and-pop restaurants scattered across the communities of southeastern Arizona:

Safford, Thatcher, Pima, Solomon, York, Clifton, Duncan, and Willcox. Visitors will find great Mexican food with the sassiest of condiments leading the way. With so many farm-fresh vegetables available, it's no surprise that the cooks are concocting some heavenly recipes. It's truly amazing what a few tomatoes, onions, and peppers can achieve when they come together and get rowdy. So grab some chips and dig in. www.salsatrail.com.

A small-town charm infuses Eastern Arizona Museum and Historical Society, spread through several rooms in what was the original bank of Pima. There's a nice collection of Native American artifacts, but the real meat of the exhibits is the pioneer displays. Everything from music boxes to firearms to colorful quilts to household items donated from families with deep roots in the community. Hours are limited due to the small volunteer staff. 2 North Main Street, Pima, 928-485-9400, www.easternarizonamuseum.com.

Tombstone Courthouse State Historic Park

Nearest Town: Tombstone.
Why Go: Relive the Wild West, right where it happened, while perusing exhibits in this stately courthouse on mining, ranching, the Apache Wars, and the most famous gunfight in history.

The click of boot heels on wooden sidewalks broke up the quiet morning. I was on Allen Street, near the spot where Buckskin Frank Leslie gunned down Billy Claiborne. A steely-eyed gent walked toward me. Suddenly, his hand flashed to his hip.

I started to duck behind a street lamp, but before I could move I saw that, instead of a six-shooter, he drew a cell phone. Whew. This place seeps into your pores.

Fast Fact: The town was originally named after the level patch of ground where the first tents and shacks went up. Wonder if there would still be the same level of fascination with the little burg if it had retained that original moniker of Goose Flats?

Two days in Tombstone and I was already dropping into a gunfighter's crouch at every sound.

The Town Too Tough to Die

Tombstone attracts Old West buffs like the Louvre draws art lovers. A trip to the West's most famous town is a pilgrimage for anyone who loves Western movies or history. Only a few places have the ability to transport you to a different time. Tombstone is one.

Yet the community itself struggles with identity issues and feels trapped between eras. A tourist destination since the 1950s when Westerns ruled the television airwaves, Tombstone was still a sleepy little burg in the '70s when I first visited. I loved

Tombstone Courthouse is where you go to separate fact from legend. Photo by the author.

it in those days. There was a certain purity about it.

It intrigued me to simply walk the streets reading the historical markers, to wander through the Bird Cage Theatre counting bullet holes (there are said to be 140), and to watch men in black frock coats stride toward the O.K. Corral and another date with destiny.

Things changed following the 1993 release of the movie *Tombstone*, starring Kurt Russell as Wyatt Earp and Val Kilmer who created the definitive charismatic Doc Holliday. The film was a modest hit in this country, a bigger one around the world, and visitation spiked. The streets of the real Tombstone were suddenly flooded and everybody wanted to be somebody's huckleberry. For a few years, Tombstone was one of Arizona's most visited destinations.

During that high-water era, Tombstone grew more commercialized as additional attractions opened and the focus of the town took a more touristy turn. It reached such a point that the National Park Service threatened to revoke the town's designation as a National Historic Landmark. A few years later, the Great Recession and the lack of Westerns coming out of Hollywood led to Tombstone's tourism numbers tumbling off a cliff.

The Real Deal

Even as the town of Tombstone struggles to find its way forward, one piece of it has remained steadfast. The Tombstone Courthouse is where you go to separate the facts from the legends.

This is the original building, one of the few structures that didn't burn down.

Fast Fact: The body count was so high during the violent years it was said that "Tombstone had a man for breakfast every morning."

A visit to Tombstone Courthouse feels a little like time travel. Courtesy of Arizona State Parks and Trails, Phoenix.

Devastating fires were just the cost of doing business in boomtowns of hastily constructed wooden buildings filled with candles and drunks. Just about every mining town went up in flames a time or two, and Tombstone was no exception.

Construction on the red brick courthouse began in 1882 just months after the Earps and Clantons swapped lead near the O.K. Corral. Built in the shape of a Roman cross, the Cochise County Courthouse became an important symbol in the wild and wooly town. The two-story Victorian courthouse held the offices of the sheriff, recorder, and treasurer, as well as the courtrooms and jail. A parade of colorful characters on both sides of the law filed through these doors.

The Founder

It all started with a tall, bearded galoot named Ed Schieffelin. Born in Pennsylvania, Schieffelin was a down-on-his-luck prospector who ended up at the newly established Camp Huachuca in 1877. When he began his search for ore in the hills across the San Pedro Valley, he was warned that all he would find was his tombstone. Apache raids were still common despite the arrival of troops.

Yet after a few months, Schieffelin found ledges of silver. In a frontier version of the clapback, he named his first claim Tombstone. And the rush was on. By 1881 Tombstone had became the largest city between St. Louis and San Francisco. That same year Cochise County was formed and Tombstone was named the county seat.

Yet all boomtowns have their bust. Water began to seep into the mine shafts. Pumps were installed but by the late 1880s the mines were flooded to the 600-foot level and could no longer be worked. Most of the residents packed up and left.

Copper mining had begun in nearby Bisbee about the same time as silver mining had in Tombstone. But it continued to flourish well after the turn of the century and beyond. (The last mine in Bisbee shut down in 1975.) Bisbee became the county seat in 1929 and all county offices were moved there.

The Tombstone Courthouse sat empty through the ensuing decades. Plans to turn it into a luxury hotel during the 1940s fizzled and it was left to deteriorate. A local group purchased the building in 1955 and began a lengthy rehabilitation project. It opened as a state park in 1959, featuring exhibits and artifacts that capture one of Arizona's most notorious chapters.

Graceful Bones

It's one of those old buildings loaded with charm and graceful bones—high ceilings, arched entryways, and spacious rooms. A winding staircase leads to the second-floor law library, courtroom, and additional exhibits.

The windows were open and a lazy breeze flowed through. Standing there in a room filled with saddles, chaps, and spurs, I heard the clip-clop of horse hooves. I glanced out the window, peering through tree leaves to watch a stagecoach roll down the street. Yeah. I was definitely in Tombstone.

Know how some museums can exhaust you? The information tends to overwhelm

Fast Fact: Although Ed Schieffelin made more than a million dollars when he sold his mining shares, he never stopped being a prospector. He traveled for a bit and even got married. But he died alone on the floor of a miner's cabin in Oregon in 1897, looking for one more strike. He's buried, per his request, in Tombstone beneath a 25-foot-tall monument shaped like the marker a miner builds when staking a claim. It is 3 miles northwest of town.

and blur together until you stagger out with eyes glazed over and less knowledge in your head than when you went in. Not the case here. The courthouse museum always fascinates me.

Maybe that's because so many of the characters have become household names. But unlike every business in town that is very singularly Earp-Clanton oriented, the museum focuses on the history of the town, the courthouse, and day-to-day life on the frontier, with informative signage accompanying an array of artifacts. It's a broader vision. Of course there's also a detailed interpretive exhibit of the Gunfight at the O.K. Corral complete with newspaper clippings and artist drawings.

There are exhibits with personal items from Wyatt Earp and from John Henry "Doc" Holliday, the Georgia dentist with a classical education who turned to gambling and drifted west after he was diagnosed with tuberculosis.

There are also displays of mining tools, medical instruments, firefighting equipment, weapons, clothing, buggies, wagons, bicycles, gambling paraphernalia, and historic photographs and documents, including an official sheriff's invitation to a hanging. Outside in the courtyard, a replica of the original gallows shows where seven men danced at the end of a rope.

In 2017 Tombstone Courthouse received a prestigious collection of Wyatt Earp memorabilia that had never been shown in public. The exhibit includes handwritten letters to Wyatt from his third wife, Josephine, handwritten notes by biographer John Flood from interviews with Earp, carbon copies of an early manuscript of the lawman's biography, wills, documents, and rare photos of Wyatt and Josephine as seniors.

After touring the courthouse, you're ready to explore the town. Despite the tourist trappings, this is still hallowed ground for history buffs. Prowl the shops along the wooden boardwalks. Read the historic markers pinpointing the locales of the carnage and mayhem that were once part of daily life. Drink in a swinging-door saloon. Listen to the clip-clop of horse hooves down the street. So much of what we think of as the Wild West occurred near where you're standing. Welcome to Arizona.

When You Go

Tombstone Courthouse State Historic Park is located at 223 Toughnut Street. It is open from 9:00 a.m. to 5:00 p.m. 520-457-3311, azstateparks.com.

Admission

Adults and youths (7–13), $. Free admission for children 6 and under.

Events

The Lighting of the Luminarias in December is one of the loveliest holiday customs in the Southwest. Luminarias began as a Spanish tradition of lighting bonfires along the roads to guide people to Midnight Mass on the final night of Las Posadas. The Las Posadas (plural form of the Spanish word meaning lodging or inn) commemorates the story of Mary and Joseph's search for a room in Bethlehem. To honor this tradition and ring in the festive season, about 225 small brown paper sacks, each filled with sand and a candle, are set out on the portico and walls for this one-night event at Tombstone Courthouse.

AROUND TOWN

The Rose Tree Festival shows off the softer side of Tombstone. Every April people flock to town to see the world's largest rose bush in full bloom. The Lady Banks rose was planted in 1885 and now covers 9,000 square feet with branches spread across a sprawling horizontal trellis. It's located in

A long simmering feud came to a bloody boil on October 26, 1881. Virgil, Wyatt, and Morgan Earp, along with Doc Holliday, squared off against Ike and Billy Clanton, Frank and Tom McLaury, and Billy Claiborne in a narrow lot near the O.K. Corral. It's still hotly debated as to who fired first.

The most famous shootout of the American West lasted 30 seconds and around 30 shots were fired. When the smoke cleared, the McLaury brothers and Billy Clanton were dead. Ike Clanton and Claiborne fled as soon as the fight commenced. Virgil, Morgan, and Holliday were wounded. Wyatt was the only participant unscathed.

Four days after the shootout, Ike Clanton filed murder charges against the Earps and Holliday. Justice of the Peace Wells Spicer convened a preliminary hearing to determine if there was enough evidence to go to trial. After a month of testimony and a parade of witnesses, Justice Spicer concluded no laws were broken.

The entire Wild West didn't take place in Tombstone, it just feels that way. Courtesy of Rick Mortensen, Cincinnati.

the courtyard of the Rose Tree Museum, a former boarding house and hotel filled with antiques and artifacts. The museum is well worth a visit any time of year.

Wyatt Earp Days takes place over Memorial Day weekend and features an 1880s fashion show, a Wyatt Earp look-alike contest, a chili cook-off, and of course plenty of shootouts.

Helldorado Days is the signature event of this iconic Western town and it's been going on for decades. It started in 1929 on Tombstone's 50th anniversary. Helldorado Days takes place the third weekend in October and features a parade, gunfight reenactments, street entertainment, live music, fashion shows, and a beard contest.

Picnic Areas

Two shaded picnic tables are available, right next to the courthouse.

Nearby Attractions

Several times a day, shots still ring out at the O.K. Corral. The reenactment of the famous gunfight provides a bit of historical context before guns start blazing. Visitors pack the bleachers to witness the spectacle that always ends with a predictable but still thrilling outburst of violence. Arrive early enough so you'll have time to tour the black-smith shop, stables, cowboy bunkhouse, and C. S. Fly's Photographic Gallery and Boarding House, where you can see Doc Holliday's room. There's also an intriguing exhibit about Tombstone's prostitutes or "soiled doves." For one last stop, visit the Historama, an old-fashioned multimedia show from 1963 narrated by Vincent Price. 520-457-3456, www.ok-corral.com.

When it comes to final resting places, none are as infamous as Boothill Graveyard. Residents include the three men who perished in the O.K. Corral gunfight, a man killed because of the color of his shirt, several men who were legally hanged, a man hanged by mistake, and the owner of the best-known grave marker of all, a Wells Fargo agent named Lester Moore, gunned down by a disgruntled customer—"HERE LIES LESTER MOORE, FOUR SLUGS FROM A .44, NO LES NO MORE." 520-457-3300, www.tombstone boothillgiftshop.com.

It's a touristy thing to do, but taking a stagecoach through the streets of Tombstone is also sort of irresistible. It feels like a way to bridge the eras between Old West and New. Two different companies offer 20-minute narrated rides throughout the day. Catch a ride with either on Allen Street in the heart of downtown. You'll pick up some interesting tidbits of information, and honestly, when are you going to get the chance to ride a stagecoach again?

Tubac Presidio State Historic Park

Nearest Town: Tubac.

Why Go: Visit the oldest European settlement in Arizona and learn the fascinating story of the presidios and missions established on the frontier of New Spain.

It's a little embarrassing to admit while surrounded by so much actual history, but my favorite part of every visit to Tubac Presidio is a modern exhibit.

A gallery of notable artwork is housed in Otero Hall. Lining the walls are 16 epic paintings by renowned Western artist William Ahrendt, each depicting an event from the state's past. The narratives were featured in an *Arizona Highways* series called "Cavalcade of History" from 1987 to 1990.

Now 16 large giclée reproductions on canvas are displayed together for the first time. They are lush, beautiful images telling a wide range of stories, such as one-armed Civil War veteran John Wesley Powell leading the first expedition down the raging Colorado River through the Grand Canyon; the caravan of camels led by Lieutenant Edward Beale as he mapped out a wagon road across the territory; and Arizona Ranger Harry Wheeler shooting it out with an outlaw in a rough-and-tumble saloon. It's a striking exhibit and I always move at a glacial pace from one to the next, soaking in the vivid action and rich details of every brushstroke. The collection is on permanent display, donated by long time Tubac resident Alan B. Davis.

Arizona's first printing press can be found at Tubac Presidio, and it still works. Courtesy of Rick Mortensen, Cincinnati.

Otero Hall was built in 1914 as a community center and used as a school in the 1930s. At many parks, that would qualify as positively historic, but by Tubac standards Otero Hall is the new kid on the block.

A Community of Firsts

Tubac Presidio State Historic Park was designated as Arizona's first state park. It preserves the original ruins of a fort, or presidio, built in 1752, making it the first European settlement in the land that would become Arizona. Visitors can study the ruins of the old fort in an underground exhibit, tour an 1885 schoolhouse, see a furnished row house from the 1890s, and investigate a museum that houses the printing press used for Arizona's first newspaper.

Tubac nestles in a green valley flanked by mountains, on the banks of the Santa Cruz River. This is a pastoral landscape of grassy plains shaggy with mesquites. Water flow in the Santa Cruz may be intermittent, but it still serves as a crucial riparian zone. Tubac sits 45 miles south of Tucson and 21 miles north of the Mexican border.

What's not immediately apparent in this peaceful setting is that Tubac was born of violence.

The Cross and the Sword

In the late seventeenth century, Spanish missionaries traveled from Mexico up the Santa Cruz River Valley attempting to Christianize the Natives. Father Eusebio Francisco Kino arrived in 1687 and began work among Indians called Pimas by the Spaniards. In their own language, they were O'odham or "the people." Kino established several missions, including Tumacácori in 1691.

Spain's empire-building policy relied on the cross and the sword. They would try at first to convert the heathens. If that failed, they resorted to force. The sword became more prominent following a 1751 revolt.

Tumacácori National Historical Park shelters the mission once protected by the Tubac Presidio. Courtesy of Rick Mortensen, Cincinnati.

The Pimas, angry over increasing Spanish controls and punishments, attacked several colonists. As a result of the rebellion, a presidio was founded at Tubac in June 1752, the first European settlement in Arizona.

The 50 cavalrymen garrisoned at the Presidio San Ignacio de Tubac were to protect the various missions in the area, quell further uprisings, and continue the exploration of New Spain. Soldiers were encouraged to bring their families with them, giving the community of Tubac an air of permanence. Indians killed the first captain of the post in 1759. The man who would become Tubac's most famous resident, Juan Bautista de Anza, assumed command.

Anza Days

Anza led numerous campaigns against the Apaches and achieved a notable reputation as a soldier and leader. However, he is best known for establishing a long-sought overland route through the desert to Alta California. Following a successful journey in 1774, Anza immediately organized a colonizing expedition for the very next year. Anza set out from Tubac with more than 240 men, women, and children on a treacherous trek of 1,800 miles that led to the establishment of the first settlement at San Francisco.

The journey to San Francisco emptied Tubac of most of its occupants. Increased Apache raids drove away others that remained. In 1776 the presidio itself was moved to Tucson. Without military protection, Tubac languished for the next decade. It wasn't until the presidio was reactivated that the community began to recover. In 1787 Spanish officers and Pima soldiers garrisoned the fort, and Tubac enjoyed a period of relative calm.

New Flags

Mexico won independence from Spain in 1821, and the new Republic of Mexico's flag flew over Tubac until 1848. That year a sudden Apache attack caused great loss of life, and months later men poured out of town, streaming for the California gold fields. Tubac was abandoned again.

Tubac was part of the Gadsden Purchase of 1853, and fortune hunters began making their way back. Charles Poston and associates formed the Sonora Exploration and Mining Company and used Tubac as their headquarters. They repaired some of the old presidio buildings and moved in. Poston, who would come to be known as the "Father of Arizona" for his role in procuring Arizona's territorial status, was the alcade of Tubac. He served as mayor, judge, town treasurer, and justice of the peace. By 1859, Tubac was the largest town in the region, and Arizona's first newspaper was established here.

When the Civil War broke out, US troops were withdrawn from Arizona to fight in the East. Tubac residents moved to Tucson and did not return until the presidio was regarrisoned in 1865 after the war.

For the next two decades—as had been the case for its entire existence—Tubac's fortunes depended entirely on military presence. This was the heart of the frontier, exposed and vulnerable, and it wasn't until the fierce Apache tribes were subdued in the 1880s that the community of Tubac stabilized.

However, it was also about the time that silver strikes led to boomtown growth in Tombstone, and the railroad was routed through Tucson, sparking that town's development. Tubac had forever lost its position of prominence.

Fast Fact: Five separate flags have flown over Tubac: Spain, Mexico, the Confederate States of America, the United States of America, and the State of Arizona.

Tubac Presidio includes several historic exhibits, including an 1885 schoolhouse. Courtesy of Rick Mortensen, Cincinnati.

An Artistic Vision

It was in 1948 that landscape painter Dale Nichols opened an art school in Tubac and the quiet little burg began an evolution into an artist colony. Today, 100+ shops are clustered in the village plaza, where old adobes, Spanish courtyards, and ocotillo fences blend seamlessly with a handful of newer buildings. There's a whiff of emergent Santa Fe here without the jostling crowds. Tubac doesn't even have a traffic light, and I found myself falling into a relaxed rhythm as I prowled the district. No wonder the town coined the slogan "Where Art and History Meet."

I got a nice lesson in the laid-back style of Tubac at The Country Shop, whose quaint adobe sits at the shady edge of the plaza. Dozens of colorful pots were stacked out front, along with planters, glassware, and patio decor. While browsing, I noticed that the shop was closed. Yet all the merchandise sat outside. A handwritten note taped to the door said, "If you want to make a purchase before we open, you may put cash or check through the mail slot. Tax is 7.6 percent. Thanks."

I'm not sure what I admire most—their

faith in human honesty or in our ability to cipher percentages.

It's easy to lose a day in Tubac. I think it's the most eclectic arts community in Arizona, with a surprisingly wide range of styles and mediums. This is the kind of place where you buy a painting for your living room, a pack of colorful greeting cards, a sculpture for the garden, and furniture for your patio. Galleries fill the historic adobes on treelined streets and spill out into hidden courtyards. Everyone leaves Tubac as an art lover.

Adjacent to the village of shops and galleries is Tubac Presidio State Historic Park. Known as Arizona's first state park (although it was the second property acquired), Tubac Presidio preserves the lengthy and multilayered heritage of the town.

The early ruins of the original 1752 presidio are still visible in an underground exhibit that was carefully excavated in 1974. Visitors will also see an impressive museum that houses an array of military exhibits, original artifacts, and interpretive displays on missions, mining, ranching, the Civil War, Arizona's territorial period, and more. The Washington printing press that printed Arizona's first newspaper is here and often demonstrated, because, yes, it still works.

The 1885 Territorial Schoolhouse is one of the oldest schoolhouses in Arizona. The Rojas House is an adobe vernacular row house built in the 1890s. Luisa Rojas was born on the property in 1894 and lived in the house until shortly before her death in 1989. The furnishings are hers. Luisa was caretaker of the schoolhouse for 30 years.

Also in Otero Hall (along with William Ahrendt's beautiful giclées) is the only 1850s ambulance on display in the United States. Outside patio exhibits show how people lived, cooked, and worked in Spanish Colonial times. Interpretive panels are located along the walking paths through the park. Living history exhibits take place most weekends fall through spring.

When You Go

Tubac Presidio State Historic Park is located about 45 miles south of Tucson. It is open from 9:00 a.m. to 5:00 p.m. One Burruel Street, 520-398-2252, azstateparks.com, www.tubacpp.com.

Admission

Adults and youths (7–13), $. Free admission for children 6 and under.

Events

Anza Days commemorates Spanish explorer Juan Bautista de Anza's 1775 expedition from Tubac to the Pacific Ocean and the founding of San Francisco. On a clear October weekend, riders in period dress equipped with shields, leather armor, and nine-foot lances engage in cavalry drills. After gathering at St. Ann's Church for a final blessing, the colorful procession rides north. The Presidio unveils their children's program with costumes, activities, props, and ponies.

AROUND TOWN

The Tubac Festival of the Arts held in February is southern Arizona's longest running art festival. Over 200 visiting artists from around the country display their work along the village streets, complementing the existing galleries. Because of the success of this event, the Fall Arts and Crafts Festival has been added to the calendar, on the first weekend in November.

Luminaria Nights are the essence of a Southwest Christmas. On one weekend in December, luminarias line the streets of the village, shops stay open late, and there's food and music. Even Santa Claus shows up to enjoy some of the magic.

Picnic Areas

There are 13 picnic tables and 5 grills located in a grove of mesquite trees.

Trails

The Juan Bautista de Anza Trail is a 4.5-mile pathway connecting Tubac Presidio State Historic Park and Tumacácori National Historical Park. The level trail traces the Santa Cruz River through shady woodlands and follows the route Juan Anza took on his expeditions. It's popular with hikers and birders.

Visitor Center

An informative video recapping the history of Tubac is shown in a small screening room. A scale model of the presidio and a few exhibits are on display. The gift shop sells a wide range of books including area histories, regional cookbooks, and wildlife guides. Souvenirs and gift items are also available. For folks strolling through Tubac's numerous galleries, there is no fee to enter the visitor center.

Nearby Attractions

Tumacácori National Historical Park protects the ruins of three Spanish mission communities. The main unit includes the Tumacácori Mission Church, which was never completed. Yet it is a profoundly moving experience to enter the sunlit sanctuary and stand in this quiet place. Behind the church is the mortuary chapel and cemetery. The visitor center contains a museum that puts a staggering amount of history in perspective. The mission is 3 miles south of Tubac, 520-377-5060, www.nps.gov/tuma.

Complete the historic timeline with a visit to the Tucson Presidio, located in the heart of downtown. In 1775 Hugh O'Conor, an Irish mercenary working for Spain, established a presidio to protect the northern frontier of New Spain. When the 11-acre fort was completed, it consisted of 10-foot-high adobe walls and two towers, each 20 feet high. The northeastern corner of the old fort has been reconstructed on its original site at Church and Washington Streets. This open-air museum, Presidio San Agustín del Tucson, provides a striking look at the city's origins. Features include a munitions room, tower, commissary, living space for soldiers, plaza, and Sonoran streetscape. Living History Days takes place the second Saturday each month from October through April with displays and reenactments of frontier life. 196 North Court Avenue, 520-837-8119, tucsonpresidio.com.

Pena Blanca Lake fills a scenic canyon just north of Nogales. Water laps at limestone bluffs and hillsides dotted with oaks. A campground and picnic areas surround the lake, which sits at 4,000 feet in elevation. As scenic as the 49-acre lake is, exercise caution when consuming fish. The lake was drained and dredged in 2008 in an effort to rid it of mercury that was accumulating in year-round fish species such as bass, crappie, and catfish. In recent years, elevated mercury levels have again been detected. Catch and release may be the way to go. 520-281-2296, www.fs.usda.gov/coronado.

Western Arizona State Parks

AMENITIES IN WESTERN ARIZONA STATE PARKS

PARKS	BOATING	CABINS	CAMPING	FISHING	HIKING	HISTORIC BUILDINGS	MOUNTAIN BIKING	PICNIC AREAS	PROGRAMS	SWIMMING
Alamo Lake	•	•	•	•				•		•
Buckskin Mountain	•		•	•	•			•	•	•
Cattail Cove	•		•	•	•			•	•	•
Colorado River						•		•		
Granite Mountain Hotshots						•				
Lake Havasu	•		•	•	•			•	•	•
River Island	•		•	•	•			•		•
Yuma Territorial Prison						•		•		•

A great blue heron surveys his domain at Alamo Lake. Photo by the author.

Alamo Lake State Park

Nearest Town: Wenden.

Why Go: Escape the hustle and bustle of everyday life at a remote scenic lake known for tournament-quality bass fishing and star-laden dark skies.

Come prepared when you venture to Alamo Lake, the most remote of all Arizona state parks.

This is the outback, the proverbial middle of nowhere. A slash of water interrupts the desert way down a dead-end road. There's nothing else around. The nearest town isn't even a town, just a dirt-road bar and burger joint (Wayside Oasis). The second nearest town is a wisp of a community strung along the highway, but that's nearly 40 miles away. Alamo Lake is a lonely, far-flung spot. That's just one more reason to go.

Off the Grid

Alamo Lake is also one of the noisiest quiet places I know. My walk along the shoreline disturbed a heron that went squawking across the lake. I listened to a couple of ravens croaking above a rock ledge. The braying of wild burros carried across the desert at sunset. I stepped out of my cabin in the evening and heard two owls hooting at each other in the darkness. When I came out later to revel in a fat, glossy moon, I wasn't the only one. Coyotes yipped from beyond the ridge. It was like some open-air karaoke joint. This is where you come when you're more interested in wildlife than Wi-Fi.

The availability of so much water in the desert is bound to make this a popular gathering spot for critters great and small, including bald and golden eagles, waterfowl, foxes, mule deer, desert tortoises, coyotes, and wild burros. The burros were first brought here by miners and turned loose when the ore played out.

Nestled in the Bill Williams River Valley, Alamo Lake is a 3,500-acre impoundment. It was created with the completion of Alamo Dam in 1968. Fed by two intermittent rivers, the Big Sandy and Santa Maria, the lake was formed to provide flood control by the US Army Corps of Engineers. Fluctuating water levels are common in the reservoir and have been known to rise 20 vertical feet in a day.

Alamo is a lanky piece of water sprawled at the feet of the Rawhide and Artillery Mountains. These are dusky ranges, sparsely vegetated. As you walk through this lean and lonely landscape, it's easy to feel like there's no one around for miles. Until you glance at the water and spy a small navy afloat.

Don't be surprised to see the lake dotted with boats. Alamo has long been regarded as one of the state's primo fishing holes, especially for largemouth bass. It is also excellent for crappie with three-pounders often being pulled from the water. Anglers can vie for bluegill, redear sunfish, and channel catfish. Fishing tournaments are regular events here.

Old Bill

The namesake of Bill Williams River is a legendary mountain man. Born in North Carolina in 1787, Bill Williams started out as a preacher and a missionary to the Osage Indians. Yet instead of converting them, Williams became enamored with their

Tucked away in the western desert, Alamo Lake is the most remote of Arizona's state parks. Photo by the author.

Wild burros are frequently seen at Alamo Lake. Photo by the author.

lifestyle and connection to the land. He married an Osage woman, but after her death he sought out more isolated places.

He survived as a trapper and was much sought after as a guide and interpreter. He was fluent in several Native American languages. Tall and gangly, with a mass of red hair and bushy beard, Old Bill, as he was known, wandered nonstop. He got along with many of the tribes, battled with others. He survived countless tough scrapes until finally he was killed by Utes in 1849.

The Bill Williams River includes the 5-mile impoundment of Alamo Lake. It flows west for another 45 miles to join the Colorado River. Near the confluence, the Bill Williams River National Wildlife Refuge protects over 6,000 acres, including one of the Colorado's last stands of cottonwoods and willows, which provides essential habitat for a variety of wildlife.

In a unique partnership, six different agencies join together with the Army Corps of Engineers to manage the water flow from Alamo Dam. Their goal is to re-create the spring flooding cycle that deposits silt and seeds on terraces above the main river channel, maintaining the health of the ecosystem. The work has paid off. Over 350 species of birds have been identified in the

Bill Williams River National Wildlife Refuge, including the endangered Yuma clapper rail and southwestern willow flycatcher.

The Big Easy

Alamo Lake is where you come to relax. Well, relax or fish. And aren't they sort of the same thing? One just requires a little more equipment and sometimes a lucky hat. The park doesn't get much day-use traffic. Anyone making the long drive to reach this peaceful place generally wants to hang around for a few nights.

Camping is plentiful in the park with about 250 sites available, including the group areas. You'll have multiple options. Choose from dry camping to full hookups, or snag one of the cozy cabins overlooking the water.

Although the cabins are basic, I enjoyed one of the best sleeps I've had in years. It was nice to be disconnected from all devices, alternating between a book and a dazzling night sky. I sacked out early and tumbled into a deep and restful slumber.

This is a BYOB park. You'll have to Bring Your Own Boat. There are no rentals. Also, if you want to unwind (responsibly, of course) with a cold beer or glass of wine, BYOB. The park store doesn't sell alcohol.

There are no official hiking trails but the burros will gladly lend you some of their routes. This is pretty gaunt terrain sitting at the edge of the Sonoran Desert and transitioning to the Mojave. So it's easy to travel cross-country, especially following some of the distinct pathways made by burros. Just keep an eye peeled for snakes.

Nearly every hilltop affords a panorama

Fast Fact: Besides the river that bears the old trapper's name, there's also Bill Williams Mountain in northern Arizona, just outside the town of, you guessed it, Williams.

of the lake. I like to ramble across the high ground for the ever-changing views. Hidden coves suddenly appear. Fingers of blue extend into the desert. Mountain reflections are captured in the shimmering water.

Yet as impressive as the daytime vistas are, the ones at night can be even more amazing. If you've not stepped away from city lights for a while, the natural night sky will startle and delight you. The diamond-studded canopy stretches from horizon to horizon, punctuated by the creamy splash of the Milky Way. It is a chance to grasp our place in the cosmos and listen for the whisper of universal secrets.

Just don't be surprised if while the universe is whispering, the burros, owls, and coyotes sing along.

When You Go

Alamo Lake State Park is located at the end of Alamo Dam Road, 37 miles north of Wenden in southwestern Arizona. 928-669-2088, azstateparks.com.

Admission

$ per vehicle (up to four adults).

Boating

There are two paved boat ramps in the park. One is located in the main campground and the other in the Cholla Campground on the northeast end of the park. There are no size restrictions on boat motors. Water skiing is permitted when water levels are high.

Cabins

Alamo Lake features four heated, air-conditioned cabins, each with two sets of bunk beds, a table, chairs, and a covered wooden porch. Bring your own bedding or sleeping bags, towels, utensils, and so on. And pack a flashlight for nighttime walks to the restrooms and showers.

Camping

There are about 250 sites including the group area spread across multiple campgrounds. Some are undeveloped, some have electric, water, and sewer, and others have just electric. All sites have a picnic table and fire ring.

Alamo Lake also sets aside a block of sites for long-term camping from October 1 through March 31. Minimum length of stay for a long-term site is 28 nights (4 weeks) and maximum is 84 nights (12 weeks).

Events

Several fishing tournaments are held at Alamo Lake during the year, with most occurring from January through April.

Each November, Alamo Lake hosts a Night Under the Stars. Far from any city lights, the park enjoys uncorrupted dark night skies. Astronomers set up telescopes to provide visitors with a closer look at the wonders of the universe. In addition, there is usually a slide presentation and solar viewing during the afternoon. Alamo Lake is a proud member of the Global Star Park Network.

Fishing

Alamo Lake contains largemouth bass, crappie, bluegill, redear sunfish, and

Cabins at Alamo Lake are perfect for those who like to rough it in style. Photo by the author.

channel catfish. A valid Arizona fishing license is required for anglers 10 years and older.

Swimming

There is no designated swimming area so make sure you swim close to shore and in full view of others. Do not swim near boat ramps, docks, or the dam. The lake's temperature can vary from temperate in the shallows to near freezing in open water. Swimmers should wear water shoes to protect their feet from hazards. In all situations, swimmers should exercise caution. There is no lifeguard on duty, so swimming is at your own risk.

Visitor Center / Store

The park store serves as visitor center. The store carries fishing and camping items such as bait, fishing licenses, boating supplies, and firewood. Groceries such as milk, eggs, canned goods, hot dogs and buns, ice cream, marshmallows, graham crackers, soda, and water are available, along with sundries and souvenirs.

Nearby Attractions

Go see the other end of the Bill Williams River, a treelined oasis, and you'll appreciate the difference made by the program of controlled flooding. The Bill Williams River National Wildlife Refuge, established to protect the vital waterway, stretches from the marshy confluence at Lake Havasu back through the lush river valley. Popular with kayakers, canoeists, bird watchers, and anglers, the refuge is 17 miles north of Parker along Arizona 95. 928-667-4144, www.fws.gov/refuge/bill_williams_river.

Alamo Lake makes a great base camp for quad riders and dirt bikers. Hundreds of miles of Off-Highway Vehicle (OHV) riding trails are located just outside park boundaries. Two trails can be accessed from the park, one from Camp Area C and

one from Camp Area E. Information is available at the visitor center. Please note that OHV use is not allowed inside the park unless the OHV is street legal.

The Wayside Oasis is located just beyond the park boundary about 3 miles down a dirt road. The combination saloon / eatery / RV park is where you can do your laundry and buy a few supplies. Places in the outback have to provide for multiple needs. But the food is good. They serve a full breakfast and some tasty burgers and sandwiches the rest of the day. You can dine inside or sit at picnic tables on the porch across from the horseshoe pits. They may be closed for much of the summer but are generally open daily in cooler months. Of course, it's always best to call ahead before venturing toward any business located down a dirt road. 928-925-3456, www.way sideoasisrvpark.com.

Buckskin Mountain State Park

Nearest Town: Parker.

Why Go: Enjoy one of the most scenic stretches along the Colorado River, with mountains on both shores cradling the curving waterway that is popular with boaters and anglers.

While heading toward the sunset, the Arizona desert comes to an abrupt end. One minute it's all stark, angled hills of rock and cacti and the next it's an expanse of blue-green water. The lower Colorado River defines much of the state's western border, creating an enticing coastline.

There may be no ocean-sized waves but Arizona's West Coast is an aquatic playground. The river unfolds in a series of lakes and wide channels as it wends its way toward Mexico. Mix in plenty of sunshine, palm trees, and circling seagulls and you

The Lightning Bolt Trail offers a panoramic view of Buckskin Mountain State Park. Photo by the author.

begin to get the picture. This is a slice of paradise for boaters, anglers, and beach bums.

Buckskin Mountain straddles a picturesque section of the Parker Strip, an 18-mile stretch of the Colorado River between Parker Dam and Headgate Rock Dam. It's an exquisite combination of stony mountains and sparkling water.

The park has two seasons. Summers belong to the river rats that show up with swimsuits, inner tubes, fishing rods, and boats of all sizes. Winter belongs to the flocks of snowbirds that arrive in a battalion of RVs. They fill the campgrounds and bask in Arizona's heavenly climate.

Is it weird that I always show up the other times? Spring and fall reveal an entirely different personality to the park. I like to roll in on the shoulder seasons when temperatures are ideal and crowds are virtually nonexistent.

Endless Summer

Late October is my favorite time to visit. By then, I'm mourning the end of summer and dreading the approach of "winter." Having grown up in the Midwest, I know how cruel a genuine winter can be. The winters I experience in Cottonwood can't even be considered cold, just chilly. But that's bad enough. I hate chilly.

So I headed for the coast where thermometers were still pushing into the upper 80s. I spent a few days suspended between desert and water, beach and cacti, until I was rejuvenated. That's one of my favorite aspects of Arizona—we always keep a little extra summer lying around if you know where to look.

Six state parks perch on the Colorado River. The two in Yuma are historic parks, but the other four are strictly for recreation.

Buckskin Mountain is a split-level park that straddles Arizona 95 nearly a dozen miles north of Parker. Buckskin makes a dramatic first impression with a sheer wall of stone rising from the water on the California shore, visible as soon as you enter.

Along the river, the park feels downright lush. A soft lawn and big shade trees surround the day-use area and campground. It's surprisingly green. A landscaped desert garden complete with tortoise habitat flanks a spacious gift shop. While there is a designated swimming zone, it can be a bit rocky. The park is also scheduled for some major renovations. Additional camping areas are planned, along with new boat-launch ramps and improvements to the park's beaches.

I lingered here at the far western edge of Arizona, dipping my toes in cool water. It's the same water that continues to carve the masterpiece of the Grand Canyon just upstream. This is some well-traveled agua overall. The Colorado River flows past a total of 11 national parks on its journey.

Lonely Saguaros

Yet I could lounge on the beach for only so long. Always the desert calls. A trio of trails leads to the other section of the park. Lightning Bolt Trail zigzags up the hillside behind the ranger station for a spectacular overview of the campground, mountains, and river.

From there visitors can access the Buckskin Trail, which crosses Arizona 95 via a pedestrian bridge. It makes a 1-mile loop through rough hills in soft earth tones that are seemingly resistant to excessive flora. Only a smattering of cacti and hardy shrubs gain purchase on the rocky slopes. A trail guide identifying the native vegetation is available at the ranger station if you want to learn more about this cast of narrow-leafed characters that always seem to look so down on their luck.

Branching off the loop are two out-and-back short paths. Interruption Point chases a ridgeline to a high perch above the highway, affording expansive views. You can see the state park nestled on the water, the road, a stretch of curving river, and a jumble of mountains spilling away. It's about a mile round trip to the point and back.

Buckskin Mountain State Park is spread along a scenic stretch of Colorado River. Photo by the author.

Another path, about half that length, visits a series of abandoned mines. Some are horizontal prospector holes, like shallow caves chiseled from hillsides. Others are small vertical shafts, now fenced off with wooden signs listing the depth of the mine and water level. They are all flooded. Apparently you didn't have to dig very deep to hit water in the Buckskin Mountains.

I don't think any of the small mines ever yielded a bonanza. But it's hard to imagine that the grizzled prospectors minded too much. These were men that spent plenty of time in the outback, and as lonely settings go, this one is tough to beat. It also begs the question, were all prospectors grizzled? Was there ever such a thing as a dapper prospector? Someone who was suave and sophisticated, too cool for a mule? And if so, whom did he have in his life to share grooming tips with?

This portion of the park feels far removed from the green riverfront. In this austere terrain, it's surprising to see the occasional saguaro growing like a sudden exclamation point. I always think of the saguaro as a sociable cactus, if there is such a thing. In more favorable habitats, they can grow in tight clumps, entire forests of them, waving their arms in the air like they just don't care.

Yet a few found their way here. They now reside far beyond their comfort zone, living like refugees in these stark hills. I wondered what brought them. Maybe they were scouting new range to expand their turf.

Or maybe they were like me, looking to add a beachy extension to their summer. They wanted to see seagulls and speedboaters and the miracle of water flowing through an unforgiving land. Maybe they

came to dip spiny toes into the Colorado River.

It was a celebration of the stunning diversity of this state. Here we stood on a scenic West Coast, my saguaros and me, and we never had to leave Arizona.

When You Go

Buckskin Mountain State Park sits 11 miles north of Parker along Arizona 95. 928-667-3231, azstateparks.com.

Admission

$$ per vehicle (up to four adults).

Boating

Buckskin Mountain offers a two-lane boat-launch ramp.

Camping

There are 80 camping and RV sites with water and electric. Some have sewer available. All sites have a BBQ grill and a picnic table. There is no limit to RV length. From April 1 through September 30 there is a two-night minimum stay for weekend camping.

Events

From January through March the park offers interpretive programs and guided hikes.

The Parker Tube Float is just what it sounds like, a river-wide party every June. A flotilla of inflatable tubes launches from Buckskin Mountain State Park and drifts downriver for 3 miles to La Paz County Park, a shorter but more scenic route than in the event's earlier, rowdier days. There's plenty of food, drink, and fun as summer officially arrives on the river.

Fishing

Largemouth and smallmouth bass, catfish, bluegill, carp, and striper are common in and around the park. A valid Arizona

---

Fast Fact: Copper was the most commonly mined ore in the area.

fishing license is required for anglers 10 years and older.

Picnic Areas

The day-use area includes a grassy lawn, plenty of shade trees, picnic tables, and grills.

Swimming

Buckskin Mountain has a designated swimming area located at the day-use area. Swimming is also allowed along the shoreline. Some areas may be rocky, so footwear is recommended. There is no lifeguard on duty. Swimming is at your own risk.

Trails

Lightning Bolt Trail is a half-mile round trip climbing to a scenic overlook.

Buckskin Trail crosses the highway via a pedestrian bridge and makes a 1-mile loop through desert hills.

Two other trails can be accessed from Buckskin: Interruption Point Trail and an unnamed path to a series of abandoned mine sites.

Nearby Attractions

Nellie E. Saloon, better known as the Desert Bar, is a far-flung outpost reached via a 5-mile rough dirt road outside of Parker. The Nellie E. occupies the site of an old mining camp, a multiterraced oasis spread across rocky hills. Everything operates by solar power and is open only Saturdays and Sundays from noon till 6:00 p.m. October through April. Bands perform throughout the day and the burgers are tender slabs of beef charred from the grill and seasoned with a fine spice of remoteness. www.the desertbar.com.

Located in a small Parker shopping plaza, the Colorado River Indian Tribes Museum contains a surprisingly diverse mix of exhibits and artworks. Four tribes are represented—the Mohaves,

Chemehuevis, Hopis, and Navajos—each with its own separate culture and traditions. Traditional and modern art is displayed, including baskets, pottery, jewelry, and kachina dolls. Learn about the history of the tribes and also about the Japanese internment camp built on the reservation during World War II. The gift shop sells authentic Native American arts and crafts and other souvenirs. 133 Riverside Drive, 928-669-8970.

Cattail Cove State Park

Nearest Town: Lake Havasu City.
Why Go: Perched on the edge of Lake Havasu, this park manages to strike the perfect balance of desert, beach, and water—offering boating and swimming fun along with miles of scenic hiking trails.

Shipwrecked. Marooned. The words flashed through my head as the sun danced across the water and the reflection sparkled like a firefly orgy.

I was a Saturday-to-Thursday Robinson Crusoe (no Friday). I was Tom Hanks without the volleyball. I was a professor and skipper shy of being Gilligan. Except unlike those other saps, I was in no hurry to be rescued.

Okay, I wasn't really stranded on a desert island. But a guy can dream, can't he? I had picked a pretty sweet spot to vanish for a while, a jut of land and a private cove. A solitary duck bobbed in the water nearby. He could be my Wilson, my Ginger, AND my Mary Ann!

Arizona is the sixth largest state in the nation, but I ran out of land in Cattail Cove. I could go no further west without boat or bridge.

Cattail Cove hugs the southern edge of Lake Havasu. This is the Arizona sea. The lake is more than a mile wide at this

A sandy beach is only one aspect of Cattail Cove. Courtesy of Arizona State Parks and Trails, Phoenix.

point—skinny by Lake Havasu standards—but still the California coast is a distant horizon of ragged mountains. No sign of humanity from where I comfortably sat.

It was achingly quiet here with only the soothing rhythm of waves lapping against the rocks. Every now and then, the hum of a motor rose as a boat knifed across open water. But neither the duck nor I tried to flag them down. We stayed happily stranded for a while longer.

Down to the Shore

Lake Havasu, formed by Parker Dam, stretches for 45 miles. It's a reservoir and a playground. Cattail Cove protects a long piece of scenic shoreline. At the end of the entrance road, a white sand beach is dotted with desert fan palms, willows, and mesquite trees. There are several shaded picnic

tables and a roped-off swim area. Plenty of shore birds can be found lounging on the beach, and they're often joined by flocks of Gambel's quail, little pear-shaped desert chickens scratching around in the sand, which always strikes me as hilarious.

A four-lane boat-launch ramp gets plenty of use. And there's even a dog beach on the south side of the ramp at the base of a hill.

The campground includes 61 sites

Fast Fact: Development began in 2017 on the former Sandpoint Marina, now known as Upper Cattail, with plans to construct additional campsites, cabins, a restaurant, a store, a marina, hiking trails, and a bridge to small islands where tent camping will be available.

Fast Fact: Wyatt Earp spent the last winters of his life working his mining claims in the Whipple Mountains.

extending back from the beach, amid shade trees and flanked by rising cliffs. If you prefer a little privacy for your own shipwreck fantasy, 32 boat-in camping sites are available.

Landlubbers will appreciate the impressive network of interconnected trails that strike out across open country. Cattail Cove offers an exquisite blend of desert and beach. Trails are spectacular, giving hikers a wide-ranging sample of terrain including beautiful lakefront, lean desert, rugged mountains, and even a rocky slot canyon.

Start by making the easy trek to Whytes Retreat. The sandy path traces the shoreline ridge south. From the elevated perch, views across the water to the Whipple Mountains in California are unceasingly beautiful.

Arizona is filled with diverse wonders but this one still manages to surprise me, year after year. It comes as a jolt, this sudden coastline. If an ideal day can be carved from a combination of sun, sky, water, and stone, you'll find it here at Cattail Cove.

It's just over a mile to Whytes Retreat, a private little beach along a curving spit of land. This is one of the boat-in campsites, but no one was here when I arrived. The beach consists of fine gravel, spiced with small white shells.

On the backside of the spit is another hidden cove. I climbed down the hill along a spine of rock poking into the water. I sat there on a sliver of bank, in that sheltered place, completely out of sight. It occurred to me that I had temporarily vanished. How nice to be marooned here for a bit, away from computers and cell phones and deadlines—just a duck bobbing nearby on gentle waves, and me. I felt a trail snooze coming on as I sprawled on the toasty rock. This

moment of utter serenity brought to you by Arizona State Parks and Trails.

But all good castaways find their way home somehow. I finally rallied, turned my back on the water, and plunged deeper into the desert.

Canyons and Hills

While I could have returned the way I came, where would the fun in that be? There are a couple of other options. Ted's Trail branches off near the campsite and cuts across the desert, scrambling over tawny hills. Vegetation is sparse through here and shade is almost nonexistent. Ted's Trail connects to another short trail, Wayne's Way. That one leads back to the beach and parking area.

I opted for the longer route on Ripley's Run. (They're big on alliteration at Cattail Cove.) Ripley's swings a wider arc through the desert as it drops into a narrow wash that squeezes between rocky walls for a long stretch. It's sort of a mini slot canyon, an intimate little defile that gives you an

The trail to Whytes Retreat follows the water's edge to a secluded cove but connects to other desert routes. Photo by the author.

up-close look at the texture of the landscape.

Don't enter the canyon if water is running or if thunderstorms are threatening—conditions that are rare in this land of reliably sunny skies. In spring, clumps of brittlebush and other wildflowers add a splash of color to an already scenic hike. .You have to navigate three dry waterfalls in the gorge, but they're fairly simple. If you can manage slightly uneven stairs, these should be no problem.

Once the trail emerges from the wash, it climbs a rocky slope and follows the crest of the hills back toward the developed portion of the park. Along the way, I enjoyed big panoramas of the lake, which seemed even more vibrantly blue when set against these mountains of chocolate and fawn and a sort of naughty beige.

It's a shade over 3 miles if you make the Whytes Retreat–Ripley's Run loop. Grab a trail map at the ranger station before starting. With a big old lake acting as your western compass point, it's hard to get lost. But not all the trail junctions have signs, so you could end up doing a little more hiking in the hills than you planned. As always, carry plenty of water. And if you plan on being "shipwrecked" in my private cove—or in one of your own discovery—take a few coconuts with you. That way you can build

Although ferocious looking, horned lizards are small and harmless. Courtesy of Arizona State Parks and Trails, Phoenix.

a recliner or bunk beds or even a radio, like the Professor did on *Gilligan's Island*.

Man, that guy could build anything out of coconuts.

When You Go
Cattail Cove State Park is located on Arizona 95 about 15 miles south of Lake Havasu City. 928-855-1223, azstateparks.com.

Admission
Admission is $$ per vehicle (up to four adults).

Boating
Cattail Cove has a four-lane boat ramp with a 10-minute courtesy dock that can accommodate any size of boat.

Camping
There are 61 camping and RV sites with water and electric, and each has a fire ring and picnic table. For holiday weekends, campers must reserve a minimum of three nights.

Cattail Cove also offers 32 primitive boat-in camping sites with picnic tables, BBQ grills, and access to pit toilets. There are waste bins, but plan to pack out your trash. Campfires are not allowed, but propane stoves are acceptable.

Events
Popular seasonal events at the park include guided hikes, moonlight hikes, and star parties with local astronomy clubs providing telescopes and instructions.

Fishing
Catch the limit of bass, catfish, bluegill, and crappie. A valid Arizona fishing license is required for anglers 10 years and older.

Picnic Areas
Shaded picnic tables are located on the beach.

Swimming

There is a designated swim area at the beach. Swimming is also allowed along the shoreline. Some areas may be rocky, especially at the boat-in campsites, so footwear is recommended. The lake's temperature can vary from temperate in the shallows to near freezing in open water. There is no lifeguard on duty. Swimming is at your own risk.

Trails

A series of trails explores the backcountry of Cattail Cove. Whytes Retreat is an easy mile-long trail that follows the water to a remote campsite and peaceful cove. All other pathways are inland routes crossing desert hills. Ted's Trail is a 0.5-mile moderate scramble across sparse terrain. Wayne's Way makes a 1-mile loop and serves as connector for the other trails. Ripley's Run is 1.9 miles through a narrow canyon before climbing a series of dry waterfalls to hilltop panoramas. Several loops of varying lengths can be created by combining different trails.

Nearby Attractions

For a glimpse at one of the most scenic sections of the Colorado River, take the Bluewater Jet Boat Topock Gorge Tour beginning in Lake Havasu City. It runs from November through May and travels through a mountainous cleft surrounded by tall cliffs and marshy shores. Keep an eye peeled for natural arches and a variety of wildlife. 928-855-7171, www.coloradoriverjetboattours.com.

On the Rubba Duck Safari, visitors pilot a two-person inflatable watercraft through Bridgewater Channel beneath London Bridge and into the open water of the lake. The guided interactive tour lasts 2.5 hours and explores the shoreline scenery and secluded coves of beautiful Copper Canyon. 928-208-0293.

Explore the water on your own. Kayaks, canoes, and stand-up paddleboards are available for rent at multiple locations in Lake Havasu City. Some rental facilities are located at the edge of the lake, while others deliver the equipment. Skimming across the water in a quiet craft, exploring the details of the shoreline, is a nice reminder that Arizona is so much more than a desert state.

Colorado River State Historic Park

Nearest Town: Yuma.
Why Go: A small park that tells the very large and important story of the Colorado River—from its wild, rowdy youth to the dangers it faces today.

Traveling from the north, you might not even recognize the mighty Colorado River in Yuma. The shallow stream meandering through town bears no resemblance to the canyon-carving, lake-filling behemoth that flows across the rest of the state.

Yet the fact that the river can be seen at all in Yuma is a minor miracle. No, strike that. A miracle implies that Yuma's remarkable transformation can't be explained. Nothing could be further from the truth. It's been the result of people with vision, unprecedented cooperation between agencies and factions, and more than a decade of hard work.

Just a few years ago, Yuma's riverfront was choked by a dense tangle of nonnative plants. Overgrown thickets of invasive tamarisk created an impenetrable barrier to the water but a favorable environment for illegal activities. The twisted jungle was cluttered with trash dumps and hobo camps, and became a popular thoroughfare for smugglers.

In the 1990s community leaders put

together a long-range plan to rescue the riverfront, which involved a massive cleanup effort, building new parks, restoring habitat, adding wetlands, designing walking and biking paths, and revitalizing downtown. Along the way they created a blueprint for other communities on how to save the most important natural resource in the American Southwest—the Colorado River.

Suddenly, that little stream looks much more significant.

The Colorado River State Historic Park occupies high ground above the water where grassy lawns are dotted with trees and walkways wind from one well-aged building to the next. For many years the park focused on an interesting but small chapter of history, back when this served as a supply point for military outposts. But Yuma always seems to be looking ahead. Once they rescued their section of river, they decided to expand their scope. In 2017 the park was renamed and rebranded with a far-reaching mission. The park exists to tell the story of the past, present, and future of the Colorado River.

River Runs Wild

Yuma exists because two granite slabs hug the Colorado River.

Before the advent of dams, the Colorado River was a volatile beast, prone to devastating floods and abrupt course changes. As it flowed through southern flatlands, the river often sprawled across 15 miles of treacherous floodplains choked with brushy marshes and patches of quicksand. Except in one spot where granite outcroppings squeezed the river through a narrow channel. This became known as the Yuma Crossing.

Fast Fact: Imperial Dam, 18 miles north of Yuma, diverts 90 percent of the remaining Colorado River water flow.

Visitors can learn the history and confront the future of a vital waterway at Colorado River State Historic Park. Photo by the author.

Europeans discovered the spot as early as 1540—some 80 years before the Pilgrims stepped off the Mayflower—when Spanish expeditions sailed up the Colorado River. Of course, they encountered established communities already on the riverbanks. These were the ancestors of the present-day Quechan and Cocopah tribes.

Father Eusebio Kino traveled through the area as he established missions in the late seventeenth century. When Juan Bautista de Anza led an expedition from the Tubac Presidio to Northern California in 1775, where he founded the city of San Francisco, he used the Yuma Crossing. During the California gold rush of 1849, tens of thousands took the rope ferry at the crossing in search of their fortunes. Fort Yuma was established in 1850 to protect the vital passageway. By the next decade, Yuma assumed a more prominent role in America's westward expansion.

Yuma Quartermaster Depot

In 1864 the US Army established the Quartermaster Depot on the high ground above the river. This compound served as a supply point for all military posts in the Southwest. River steamboats delivered goods to the depot, where a six-month supply of ammunition, food, and clothing was maintained. From here materials were shipped north on river steamers or overland by mule wagons.

For most of the next two decades, the depot provided lifelines to army posts scattered across Arizona, Nevada, Utah, New Mexico, and Texas. The arrival of the Southern Pacific Railroad in 1877 changed things. Trains could transport supplies faster and cheaper. The Quartermaster Depot closed in 1883.

The site stayed active as a telegraph and weather station and customs office. The Bureau of Reclamation made this their first home. Engineering pioneers worked from here to build dams to prevent floods, generate power, and ensure a source of water. It allowed the Southwest to flourish but came with a high cost.

Colorado River State Historic Park includes many buildings that once served as the Quartermaster Depot during the era of riverboats. Photo by the author.

One Dam Thing after Another

The dams caused serious impact to the river's ecology. Without the annual cycle of spring floods, forests along the riverbanks died out. Marshes and wetlands turned into parched desert. Birds and wildlife packed up and went looking for more suitable habitat. Invasive species like salt cedar, also known as tamarisk, sunk roots in the degraded ecosystem and quickly took over.

After decades of neglecting the very reason for its existence, the city of Yuma began to change course. The Yuma Crossing National Heritage Area began implementing its master plan in the early 2000s. They renovated and reopened the historic Ocean to Ocean Bridge in 2002. That same year, West Wetlands Park was unveiled. What had been a huge dumping ground now featured picnic ramadas, grassy lawns, a lake, a hummingbird garden, and a giant playground designed by families.

The crown jewel of the project, the East Wetlands opened in 2004. The pioneering restoration project cleared over 400 acres of invasive species, replacing them with more than 200,000 cottonwood, willow, and mesquite trees. The project formed a back channel to create a marsh and employed some flood-control techniques to fool the native trees into believing it's just like it was 150 years ago. Birds have returned in force, including the endangered Yuma clapper rail.

A New Beginning

Colorado River State Historic Park is the latest incarnation of the lovely 10-acre park perched on a bluff overlooking the river. It had been known as the Yuma

Quartermaster Depot, honoring that chapter of Yuma's history. When it was rebranded in 2017, it was one more step in Yuma's continuing growth to find ways to preserve and protect this vital resource.

Some of Arizona's oldest buildings are found on this patch of high ground above the floodplain. Each structure is filled with artifacts and displays. The Quartermaster Depot era is still represented. So is John Wesley Powell, the one-armed Civil War veteran who led the first expedition down the river through the Grand Canyon.

There's an impressive exhibit about the Yuma Siphon, a massive tunnel under the Colorado River that first delivered irrigation water to the valley in 1912, and still operates today, right next to the park. It was this engineering marvel that allowed Yuma's agricultural industry to flourish. Today, Yuma grows more than 90 percent of the nation's leafy vegetables consumed from November to March.

A small theater shows several short films throughout the day that look at the river from different perspectives. One wall-sized chart tracks where all the river water goes. Other displays examine the benefits and environmental impacts of dams. A Colorado River research library may be used by appointment. And bonus: there's even an old-time pie shop that dishes up some tasty desserts during the cooler months.

One striking thing about the park exhibits is that they ask almost as many questions as they answer. It's clear the goal here is to spark a dialogue about the stresses faced by the Colorado. This snowmelt-fed river is a vital source of water for 40 million people and that number continues to grow.

My Two Cents

For a long time, I hated Yuma. That was my first, second, and probably my third impression. It was just about the only place in this amazing state that I couldn't tolerate.

Here was a desert town blessed with a river, which it completely ignored. That infuriated me.

Then a funny thing happened. After years of actively avoiding the dump, I showed up again in 2010. And I couldn't believe what I was seeing. What once looked like a weed-choked, garbage-strewn culvert was a new, gleaming riverfront. Parks with sandy beaches, shady forests, and walking paths stretched for miles. I could see actual flowing water and cattail-lined marshes with ducks and egrets splashing about. The once-deserted downtown was bustling with shops, eateries, and museums. Agritourism was booming. A convoy of gourmet food trucks lined the roads. It had turned into a vibrant town, great for travelers.

I've been back every year since. It's become one of my favorite road trips. I'll say without hesitation that Yuma is the poster child for doing things right—for putting together a comprehensive, long-term vision and then following through. They completely won me over.

The establishment of the Colorado River State Historic Park is just another example of the town facing up to current and future challenges and trying to find a way to overcome them.

When You Go

Colorado River State Historic Park is located at 201 North Fourth Avenue. It is open from 9:00 a.m. to 5:00 p.m. Park exhibits close at 4:30 p.m. Closed Mondays June through September. 928-783-0071, azstateparks.com.

Fast Fact: Yuma is the sunniest place on Earth, receiving over 4,000 hours of sunlight per year, more than any other city.

Admission

Adults and youths (7–13), $. Free admission for children 6 and under.

Bike Rentals

Bicycles are available by the hour or the day for those that want to take advantage of the miles of trails that stretch along Yuma's riverfront, connecting West Wetlands, Gateway Park, and East Wetlands. All are easily accessed from the Colorado River State Historic Park.

Events

AROUND TOWN

If you want to sample a culinary range of what Yuma has to offer, Savor Yuma tours are for you. These gastronomic adventures are progressive dinners where participants shuttle from one local eatery to the next, experiencing everything from food trucks to fine dining. Participants are transported by motor coach, stopping at three different restaurants. Savor Yuma tours run through winter into early spring.

The Somerton Tamale Festival is the Woodstock of tamale events, with over 30,000 people descending on the little border town south of Yuma. Visitors will have the chance to sample dozens of tamale varieties ranging from traditional beef and chicken to pork, turkey, corn, and spinach. There are even some sweet tamales filled with pineapple, peach, or strawberry. The annual festival takes place in December, with all proceeds helping to provide Arizona State University scholarships to local students.

Picnic Areas

Picnic tables are located near many of the historic buildings.

Visitor Center

The visitor center of the park also serves as the information center for the Yuma Visitors Bureau, providing numerous brochures, guides, and maps. There are a few exhibits and a theater where various movies about the Colorado River are shown throughout the day. The gift shop sells T-shirts, souvenirs, toys, magnets, and a good selection of books.

Nearby Attractions

Yuma's riverfront parks are an inspiring testament to what communities can accomplish when they work together. Just a few years ago, the river was cluttered with trash dumps and hobo camps. Today, the West Wetlands features a small lake, a hummingbird garden, a burrowing owl habitat, and a spectacular family-friendly playground that kids call Castle Park. Downtown Gateway Park offers sandy beaches and picnic ramadas. East Wetlands has been restored to a natural balance, with a forest of cottonwoods and grassy marshes. Paved and lighted trails trace the river and connect all three parks. www.visityuma.com.

Glean a sense of how all the historic pieces of Yuma fit together with a visit to Pivot Point Interpretive Plaza. The outdoor exhibit overlooks the river and Gateway Park at the end of Madison Avenue, the exact location where the first train chugged into the Arizona Territory in 1877. A 1907 Baldwin locomotive marks the spot, near the concrete pivot from the old swing-span rail bridge. Colorful panels recount all the chapters of Yuma's past. And if you want to climb into the engineer's seat of the Baldwin and pretend you're at the controls of the big brute, it's cool.

Halloween comes early when you ride the Ghost Trolley Tours of Historic Yuma. Hop aboard and roll through Yuma's downtown district. Along the way you'll be regaled with tales of murder and mayhem from Yuma's surprisingly rowdy past. You'll also make a nighttime visit to the spooky Pioneer Cemetery, which is guaranteed to

bring out the goosebumps. Tours take place on specific dates from January through April. The trolley leaves from the Sanguinetti House Museum and Gardens, a great place to delve into Yuma's rich history. 928-782-1841, www.arizonahistorical society.org.

Granite Mountain Hotshots Memorial State Park

Nearest Town: Yarnell.
Why Go: Pay tribute to the 19 brave firefighters who gave their lives battling the Yarnell Hill Fire amid these rugged mountains.

It's surprising what gets to you. Certainly the plaques are poignant, but I knew that going in.

What hit me hard were the trees. At first I passed along brushy, boulder-punctuated slopes, green as could be in the early days of autumn. There was no sign that a fire ever swept through here—until about a half mile up the switchbacks. Then I noticed a handful of small bare trees surrounding me on the trail. The slender trunks still bore scorch marks, and I suddenly choked up.

Granite Mountain Hotshots Memorial State Park pays tribute to the 19 elite wildland firefighters who died on June 30, 2013, while battling the Yarnell Hill Fire.

Yarnell perches on the high shoulder of the Weaver Mountains at an elevation of 4,800 feet. A discovery of gold first put the town on the map, but it grew into a ranching community as well as a pastoral little getaway for desert dwellers. The highway

A view from the Hotshots Trail shows the town of Yarnell and the final route taken by the 19 Granite Mountain Hotshots. Photo by the author.

makes a long winding drive up Yarnell Hill from the cactus-dotted lowlands far below.

The state park overwhelms you right from the start. The entrance is nothing more than a highway pullout for a handful of vehicles snugged up against a mountain slope towering overhead. A couple of parking slots are set aside for folks who are unable to hike the trails but still want to pay their respects. There's a lovely life-sized bronze statue of a wildland firefighter. Signs are posted with details of the park, a timeline of that fateful day, names and photos of the men who perished, and one photo guaranteed to poke you right in the heart.

Fast Fact: The Yarnell Hill Fire caused the largest loss of firefighters' lives since the September 11 attacks.

It's the Hotshots crowded around a gigantic alligator juniper tree—in fact, the world's largest alligator juniper. The crew is dirty and sooty and wearing wide grins. Besides protecting many high-end homes, they had saved the iconic tree from the Doce Fire, which had blazed on the outskirts of Prescott, where they were stationed. They look so young.

Just 11 days after the photo was taken, the Granite Mountain Hotshots answered the alarm for a small fire burning outside the town of Yarnell.

Hotshots Trail

For those of us making the hike, a metal staircase boosts us over a sheer wall of rock and onto the Hotshots Trail. This path scrambles up the steep slope of the Weaver Mountains. This is a serious trail, a

reminder of the type of terrain that wildland firefighters often had to navigate while toting chainsaws and shovels and 50-pound packs. It makes a 1,200-foot climb in a series of sharp switchbacks weaving between clusters of boulders. Along the way, 19 granite plaques are set into stones, each telling the story of one of the men.

The climb is steady and relentless with views expanding the higher you go. In many places, steps are cut into the rocks. A few benches are placed at strategic locations along the way. The trail finally begins to level out after 2.5 miles following a ridgeline toward an observation deck. As I hiked the ridge, I was walloped by the biggest jolt of all.

I had always retained this image that the Hotshots met their end in some isolated spot, far from everything. But I could gaze down at the fatality site some 400 feet below, and not far beyond was a swath of cleared space and the distinctive outline of a ranch. They were so close to safety, so damn close. It devastated me.

The Observation Deck marks the end of the Hotshots Trail. There's a sheltered bench here and detailed signs with maps and timelines of how events unfolded.

The Fire

On June 28, 2013, lightning ignited a small wildfire on BLM lands above Yarnell. It burned slowly in rough terrain at first, but strong winds caused the fire to spread to 2,000 acres by June 30 amid triple-digit temperatures. The craggy slopes were thick with chaparral, impassably dense and tinder dry.

The 20-man team of Granite Mountain Hotshots hiked into the Weaver Mountains on the morning of June 30 to the southeast corner of the blaze to build a fire line, cutting brush to deprive the fire of fuel. Winds were blowing out of the south, pushing the fire north away from the Hotshots and toward the ranching community of Peeples Valley.

After lunch, the Hotshots posted a lookout on higher ground to monitor the fire and weather conditions. As the afternoon grew hotter and a storm system developed with strong, gusty winds, the fire increased in intensity and began to behave erratically. Flame lengths grew and dark smoke filled the sky.

Suddenly, winds shifted 180 degrees, pushing the flame front toward Yarnell. Soon afterward the lookout was forced to abandon his position. The fire gained speed and a sudden frantic evacuation of Yarnell began with people fleeing homes just ahead of roaring flames. The other 19 Granite Mountain Hotshots began descending from the ridge through a shallow canyon.

This is the part that's difficult to understand. The Hotshots were out of danger. They were in the black, that area of vegetation that had already been burned. They could have stayed put and stayed safe. So why then did they start down through a box canyon choked with fuel?

While there's no way to know for certain, it seems most likely they simply wanted to do their job. They knew that the flames were racing toward Yarnell and that residents were being evacuated and fire crews were being pulled out. Instead of staying on the sidelines and watching the town burn, they chose to do what they always do—try to make a difference. If they could reach the cleared space of the ranch, a designated safe zone on the edge of Yarnell, they would be in a position to reengage the fire, maybe save some homes.

Once the Hotshots were in the canyon traveling roughly parallel to the fire, they

Visitors can hike to the fatality site at Granite Mountain Hotshots Memorial State Park and pay their respects. Photo by the author.

could no longer see the blaze. They didn't realize it had shifted direction again and had dramatically increased in speed. A wall of flames suddenly turned into the east end of the canyon, trapping the men. Their last radio communication came at 4:41 p.m., indicating that they were attempting to deploy their emergency shelters.

All wildland firefighters carry the shelters—thin silver cocoons of aluminum foil, woven silica, and fiberglass. They're designed to deflect radiant heat but can't withstand direct contact with flame. Firefighters deploy shelters only as a matter of last resort.

Journey Trail

The Observation Deck also marks the beginning of the 0.75-mile Journey Trail that traces the final route taken by the Hotshots. They descended from the ridge into the canyon. The angle is steep at first before moderating.

As I got lower, I noticed the boulder-strewn hill on the north side, now blocking my view in that direction. This is where the

Hotshots would have lost sight of the fire as they made their way through the scratchy tangle of chaparral that was 10 feet tall in places at that time. Near the mouth of the canyon, just as the ground levels, with the ranch buildings just a few hundred yards away, sits the fatality site.

Here 19 chain-linked gabions—large stone-filled mesh baskets—encircle the small site. Within the circle are 19 crosses clustered in tight groups, marking where each man was found. No one broke off. They stayed together, working as a team until the very end. Each cross bears a name and the date, June 30, 2013.

Like most people in Arizona, I didn't know any of the Hotshots. But like just about everybody in the state, I feel a powerful kinship. It's hard to explain but they became sons and brothers for us all. I paid my respects and then hiked out.

Experience the Beauty

Even though it's a hike tinged with sadness, I made a point to do what I do on all trails. I savored the vistas, I greeted lizards, admired wildflowers, ran my hands over the rough skin of boulders, and just generally reveled in the wonders of the day. To do any less would have been disrespectful to these heroic young men.

They chose their career to help others, to be outdoors, and to make a difference with their lives. I believe they would want that legacy to continue. And those scorched trees that hit me so hard when I first saw them? On the way back I stopped to notice all the new growth, a few feet tall coming from the base. Life goes on.

These will be trails that attract many nonhikers. Some folks who may not spend a lot of time scrambling up mountainsides

---

Fast Fact: The Yarnell Hill Fire burned a total of 8,400 acres.

will still want to visit these particular trails. I totally understand that.

If you hike all the way to the fatality site and back, it's a total of 7 miles. And those are mostly strenuous miles. Be prepared. Wear adequate footwear, a hat, and plenty of sunscreen. Carry lots of water and some salty snacks. Hike with family or friends if possible and make sure someone knows your itinerary.

And don't feel like you need to hike the whole way. There are benches placed along the trail at several spots. The first one shows up just before the second plaque, about a quarter mile up the trail. It's a lovely spot to ponder the views, read the stories of a couple of brave men, and get a nice half-mile round-trip workout.

Or maybe you can make it to the second bench. Or the third. Or to the very end. The important thing is to stay safe, enjoy some Arizona beauty, and spend a little time honoring the spirits of some remarkable men.

When You Go

Granite Mountain Hotshots Memorial State Park is located 2 miles south of Yarnell on southbound Arizona 89. Parking is limited, so during busy times visitors are urged to carpool or to make arrangements with a shuttle service beforehand. The park is open from sunrise to sunset. azstateparks.com.

Admission

Free.

Trails

The Hotshots Trail is a strenuous 2.85-mile path ascending 1,200 feet through the Weaver Mountains. Hikers will encounter over 200 stairs along the way. The trail ends at the Observation Deck overlooking the fatality site. A tribute wall, bench, and interpretive signs are here.

The Journey Trail allows hikers to follow in the last steps of the Hotshots, descending

0.75 miles to the fatality site some 400 feet below on the canyon floor.

Nearby Attractions

A renewal of spirit is offered at the Shrine of St. Joseph of the Mountains in Yarnell. Built in 1939, life-sized sculptures representing the Last Supper, the Garden of Gethsemane, and the Crucifixion are spread through the shaded grotto of oak trees and granite boulders. Visitors can walk a winding trail over the hilly terrain through the Stations of the Cross, or meditate in the park-like setting. The shrine lost a few buildings in the Yarnell Hill Fire but largely survived intact. 16887 West Shrine Drive.

Lake Havasu State Park

Nearest Town: Lake Havasu City.
Why Go: This scenic shoreline with white sand beaches, swaying palm trees, and sparkling water is the very definition of Arizona's West Coast.

I was kayaking through Topock Gorge when I had my first piranha sighting.

Part of the Havasu National Wildlife Refuge, Topock Gorge cradles a writhing, twisted section of the Colorado River. This stretch of water at the upper end of Lake Havasu was cursed by riverboat captains back in the days of big paddle-wheelers, which explains how one especially treacherous bend acquired the name Devil's Elbow. The cliffs of the narrow gorge, carved into oddly tilted hoodoos, jagged spires, and keyhole arches, enhance the drama of the journey.

As I drifted past one peaceful cove, an explosion of shrieks and screams ripped apart the morning silence. There was a furious thrashing in the water and blood sprays streaking the side of a boat. Then someone yelled, "Cut!"

Lake Havasu State Park is the very definition of Arizona's West Coast. Courtesy of Arizona State Parks and Trails, Phoenix.

They were filming *Piranha 3D*, and I got to witness some of the carnage. At the time, it was being kept quiet that crews were shooting here. No one wanted to give the impression that there are actually piranhas in Lake Havasu. That was a very real concern. So just to clarify, if piranhas occupied the Colorado River, I would not.

Shockingly, despite the fact that my calm demeanor allowed the scene to go off unimpeded, I did not receive an executive producer credit for the film.

A Bridge to Cross

At nearly 11,000 acres, Lake Havasu State Park is by far the largest of Arizona's West Coast parks. And located right in the heart of Lake Havasu City, just upstream from London Bridge—yes, *the* London Bridge—it's also the busiest.

Fast Fact: Lake Havasu City founder Robert P. McCulloch purchased the London Bridge in 1968 for the tidy sum of $2,460,000. It was disassembled, shipped overseas to California, and delivered by truck to Lake Havasu City where it was reconstructed and rededicated in 1971.

There's a curious overlapping of cultures here that always intrigues me. This place draws a mix of beach bums, anglers, RVers, and snowbirds. They're all hanging out near London Bridge, which spans a channel of water in the Arizona desert. And that big antique attracts large numbers of international visitors. Yet they all make way in March and April for the swarms of youthful partiers that arrive at the balmy lake to celebrate spring break.

Lots of different tribes, lots of different needs. Somehow they all find what they're looking for on the shore of Lake Havasu. There has always been something magical about a community conjured up in a remote corner of the desert by a visionary who was just looking for a place to test his outboard motors.

Robert P. McCulloch purchased 26 square miles of lakeside property in 1963. The successful businessman was already known for his chainsaws but he also ran McCulloch Motors, the same ones he was testing in the sparkling blue lake.

Prospective property buyers were flown in at no charge to look at this middle-of-nowhere spot where McCulloch expected to build a city. There was only one paved street at the time. To spur growth in the fledgling city, he opened a chainsaw manufacturing plant in 1964. A few years later he decided Lake Havasu City needed an attraction so he purchased that little bauble in old London town.

Arizona's Beachfront Property

Lake Havasu State Park defines Arizona's West Coast. The look, the feel, the attitude is all there. It's an idyllic combination of

Lake Havasu makes a dandy perch for sunset views. Photo by the author.

Fast Fact: The vintage lamps on the London Bridge are made from the melted-down cannons of Napoleon Bonaparte's army.

water, sand, swaying palm trees, and seagull wings flashing white in the sun. The park stretches along the shoreline. Many of the campsites are almost right at the water's edge.

There's only one trail, the Mohave Sunset Trail that meanders across the park. It curves through desert scrub, past the Arroyo-Camino Interpretive Garden, tracing the shoreline, and finally tops a low hill overlooking the lake. Brushier vegetation here makes this a popular spot for birders.

Over 175 species of bird have been recorded in the park.

Yet it's iconic Windsor Beach that's the centerpiece of the property. The long, wide belt of white sand is dotted with big palm and twisted mesquite trees. It's a great gathering spot in any season. Covered picnic tables and restrooms anchor the day-use area, but the beach continues past the campground and boat ramps. Set back from the water is a grassy area that's popular for holding special events.

Windsor is also an astonishing sunset-viewing perch, combining the best of desert dusks and ocean twilights. Arizona is known for consistently brilliant sunsets. Lack of pollution and humidity are factors. High clouds common to our arid climate

A day at Lake Havasu ends with a flourish. Courtesy of Arizona State Parks and Trails, Phoenix.

Water, beaches, and lighthouses are not your typical Arizona scene. Photo by the author.

create the perfect reflectors for the intense colors. So the stage is already set when the sun makes a last gasp and bathes the horizon in wondrous light. Then add an expanse of water to mirror everything that's going on in the sky as it cycles through a rainbow of vivid hues—lemon, orange, tangerine, and plum—and it's like standing in the middle of a roaring, raging citrus fire. It's a show not to be missed.

Shine Your Light on Me

At the edge of the beach in the day-use area, overlooking the London Bridge Channel, you may notice a lighthouse. This is one of 26 that encircle the lake. And don't be deceived by their adorably cute size.

Fast Fact: Habitat restoration seems to be paying dividends around the lake. The threatened northern Mexican garter snake, which had not been seen along the lower Colorado River for decades, started returning in 2015 to the Havasu National Wildlife Refuge and the Bill Williams National Wildlife Refuge.

These are all working navigational systems, helping to keep boaters safe.

Each is a scaled-down version of one of America's most famous lighthouses. Replicas of East Coast lighthouses line the east side of the lake and ones from the West Coast are re-created on the western shore. Built and maintained by the Lake Havasu Lighthouse Club, each of the small structures is about 1/3 the size of the originals.

The one in Lake Havasu State Park is a replica of the East Quoddy Lighthouse. The original is perched on Campobello Island in New Brunswick, Canada. A map to all the lighthouses is available at the Lake Havasu City Visitor Center.

When You Go

Lake Havasu State Park is located at 699 London Bridge Road. 928-855-2784, azstateparks.com.

Admission

$$ per vehicle (up to four adults).

Boating

The park has four boat ramps. There are no size restrictions.

Boat rentals are available through the park's concessionaire, Wet Monkey Powersport Rentals. 928-855-2022, www.wetmon keyrentals.com.

Camping

There are 47 sites with water and electric, each with a fire ring and picnic table. Most sites can accommodate RVs and tents. Additional campsites are planned. From April 1 through September 30 there is a two-night minimum stay for weekend camping.

Events

In January, the Havasu Balloon Festival and Fair creates a colorful spectacle and is now held in the park. Dozens of hot-air balloons fill the skies, wafting above the shimmering lake in a graceful kaleidoscopic extravaganza. There are mass ascensions each day, weather permitting. Also included are carnival rides and games, food vendors, tethered balloon rides, skydivers, live music, lovely balloon night glows, and plenty more.

Every March, Bluegrass on the Beach takes place in the park, where that high lonesome sound shakes the fronds of palm trees and skips across the water. The event brings out a mix of big-name bands and energetic newcomers alike. There are jam sessions, workshops, and arts and crafts, as well as beer, food, and a kid zone. Don't forget lawn chairs and blankets.

AROUND TOWN

The Boat Parade of Lights that takes place every December is one of Arizona's most unique holiday parades. Dozens of brightly decorated boats cruise the Bridgewater Channel and pass under London Bridge in a glimmering spectacle that sets the water ablaze. There are several good viewing spots in the park.

Fishing

Fish commonly caught in the lake are smallmouth bass, largemouth bass, striped bass, and various catfish and sunfish species. A valid Arizona fishing license is required for anglers 10 years and older.

Picnic Areas

Picnic tables, shade ramadas, grills, restrooms, and water are available at Windsor Beach.

Swimming

Lake Havasu State Park has a large designated swimming area located at Windsor Beach. Swimming is allowed elsewhere along the shoreline, but certain areas may be rocky. Do not swim near boat ramps or docks. The lake's temperature can vary from temperate in the shallows to near freezing in open water. There is no lifeguard on duty. Swimming is at your own risk.

Trails

The Mohave Sunset Trail winds its way through lowland desert and along the shoreline for 1.75 miles.

Nearby Attractions

If you want to get the whole story on how the London Bridge ended up in the Arizona desert, sign up for a walking tour offered by the visitor center. Learn not just about the stone and concrete structure but also about its storied history. See the strafing scars from World War II and hear about the mysterious ghosts that still haunt the bridge. The 90-minute tour is conducted October through April, covers a half mile, and climbs 51 steps. 422 English Village, 928-855-5655, golakehavasu.com.

Since no Lake Havasu City existed before 1963, you'd think a museum might be thin on exhibits. But Lake Havasu Museum of History maintains a surprising collection on the Chemehuevi tribe, mining, riverboating, Parker Dam, London Bridge, and the development of Lake Havasu City. 320 London Bridge Road, 928-854-4938, havasumuseum.com.

Sunset Charter and Tour Company takes small groups out on the *Serenity Now* at the end of the day for a sunset outing. Cruise past well-known landmarks such as Balance Rock, Sleeping Indian, Copper Canyon, and Steamboat Cove on this narrated tour. Enjoy a lavish display as the setting sun illuminates surrounding mountains and streaks the lake with color. Since group size is limited to six, reservations are strongly recommended. You can also schedule a trip through Topock Gorge. Watch out for piranhas. 928-716-8687, www.lakehavasuboattours.com.

Wedge Hill Trail shows off some grand views of River Island State Park.
Photo by the author.

River Island State Park

Nearest Town: Parker.
Why Go: Nestled in a sheltered cove on the Colorado River, visitors enjoy an intimate connection with the water and the mountains rising along the shore.

I'm an idiot. River Island just proves it.

I had always bypassed this little park that sits just over a mile north of Buckskin Mountain, pegging it as only a campground for river rats and snowbirds. Well, it is that but it's also much more.

River Island is a speck of a park, nestled in a small sloping bowl at the base of stark mountains that rise from the river's edge. The setting snatches your breath, and with only 37 campsites, this is about as intimate an experience with the river as you can get.

Of those campsites, 8 are beachfront real estate, sitting on a grassy lawn just beyond the water and ideal for tents. The park has a sheltered sandy beach and a three-lane boat ramp, and that's pretty much the extent of the amenities.

Short but Sweet

What always kept me away was the lack of trails. The only option seemed to be Wedge Hill Trail, a half-mile path. But holy hiking boots! This runt of a path is absolutely worth the stop. It's among the most beautiful half miles in the state park system.

Starting from beside the boat launch ramp, Wedge Hill scrambles up into the bluffs overlooking a sharp bend in the river. The views are absolutely mesmerizing, with the sun glinting off the blue-green water, framed by a cluster of craggy mountains.

The cliffs surrounding River Island catch the last rays of an autumn sun.
Photo by the author.

There are a few well-placed benches early on where you can sit and admire the dramatic panoramas.

The trail wiggles up the slopes freckled with a few cactus varieties. This is hard-edged country, bare rock and sharp angles. The vistas seem to change every few steps as more of the river is revealed and mountains rise up behind you. There's no shade so be wary in the summer heat.

Joined at the Highway

Up top the pathways meander off in a few different directions, but they're all dead ends at different overlooks. You'll have to return the way you came. But I didn't mind checking out the various perspectives before I climbed back down because these are all memorable panoramas—plenty of high cliffs, desert mountains, and a winding river mixed with clusters of beachfront homes on the California side. One route even leads out to the road. Keep this in mind because plans are in the works to create a trail along the east side of Arizona 95 to connect River Island and Buckskin Mountain, which I'm very excited about.

River Island began as a detached unit of neighboring Buckskin Mountain. While they're considered separate parks today, they're still closely connected, sharing staff and the visitor center at Buckskin.

While Buckskin Mountain is a larger, more bustling park—with plans for additional growth—River Island is small, less developed, and quieter. That holds strong appeal to many visitors. I just happen to be one of them.

Fast Fact: La Paz County was formed in 1983, making it the only county created after Arizona achieved statehood in 1912. Parker is the county seat.

When You Go

River Island State Park is located just over a mile north of Buckskin Mountain State Park, about 12 miles north of Parker at 5200 North Arizona 95. 928-667-3386, azstate parks.com.

Admission

$$ per vehicle (up to four adults).

Boating

The boat ramp is three lanes, launching in a calm cove. The cove is a no-wake zone. Be alert. An island reef is located in the center of the cove. Hug the cliffs to access the main river channel. Observe all navigational aids (buoys).

Camping

There are 37 sites. The 8 beachfront sites on the grass are ideal for tents and small campers up to 24 feet. The other sites can handle larger RVs up to 65 feet, and include electric and water. From April 1 through September 30 there is a two-night minimum stay for weekend camping.

Events

AROUND TOWN

During February, a miniature city springs up on the fringe of Parker as participants, support crews, and spectators gather for a huge old-fashioned off-road race. The Parker 425 sends hundreds of trucks and buggies careening across the desert, a wild, sand-lashing spectacle.

Fishing

Largemouth and smallmouth bass, catfish, bluegill, carp, and striper are common in and around the park. A valid Arizona fishing license is required for anglers 10 years and older.

Picnic Areas

The park has a large shaded ramada with lights, an electrical outlet, and water.

Swimming

River Island is a popular swimming spot. A sandy beach spans the riverfront, which is tucked away in a cove and protected from the river's current. There is no lifeguard on duty. Swimming is at your own risk.

Trails

The 0.5-mile Wedge Hill Trail climbs into the hills above the Colorado River.

Nearby Attractions

In 1909 Swansea had a population of 500. It was abandoned a few years later and today is slowly succumbing to the elements. But there's still plenty to see for history buffs. Nestled among sparse desert hills far from any hint of civilization, the former copper town is a picturesque panorama of ruin. Several crumbling adobes are visible, along with the remnants of the railroad depot, rows of miners' quarters, two cemeteries, and mine shafts. The BLM manages the Swansea Townsite, about 25 miles east of Parker, and has added an interpretive trail, picnic tables, and a camping area. Some travel is on a dirt road, and high-clearance vehicles are recommended. 928-505-1200.

Some 35 miles south of Parker, Quartzsite is a throwback, keeping the tradition of frontier boomtowns alive—except that the boom/bust cycles are a seasonal loop. The ramshackle little outpost exists as a few businesses strung along the interstate until winter, when hordes of snowbirds descend—slowly, with turn signals ablaze. For three months the surrounding desert resembles a network of RV dealerships, and Quartzsite sprouts hundreds of food trucks, kiosks, and vendor stalls. This sunbaked corner of the desert becomes one of the world's largest open-air flea markets. It's a rock hound's paradise with several gem shows, arts and crafts festivals, and ongoing swap meets that attract additional day-trippers to the town. 928-927-5200, www.quartzsitetourism.com.

Yuma Territorial Prison State Historic Park

Nearest Town: Yuma.

Why Go: Explore the eerie remains of the Old West's most notorious penitentiary, where the cellblocks, guard towers, and infamous "Snake Den" still overlook the Colorado River.

While I was not a fan of Yuma for many years (see Colorado River State Historic Park for my grievances), the attraction that always brought me back was the prison. There was a gritty reality to it that fascinated me. Also, I think I'm intrigued by any prison that I'm not in. It validates my life choices somehow.

Long before Alcatraz was called the Rock, Yuma Territorial Prison actually was one. On July 1, 1876, the first seven inmates moved into cells they themselves had hacked from the granite hill above the Colorado River.

Over the next 33 years, the prison would earn a fearsome reputation. A total of 3,069 prisoners, including 29 women, lived inside the walls. They were convicted of a wide range of crimes that included murder, assault, grand larceny, adultery, selling liquor to Indians, forgery, mayhem, prizefighting, and having too many wives. The youngest inmate was 14 while the oldest was 88. Mexican revolutionaries were jailed along with prominent Mormon leaders. Some of the prison's most notable inmates included "Buckskin" Frank Leslie, whom Wyatt Earp compared to Doc Holliday in gun skill; Pearl Hart, who committed the last Arizona stagecoach robbery; and spooky-eyed Elena Estrada, who allegedly stabbed her unfaithful lover and then cut open his chest, pulled out his heart, and

The cellblocks of Yuma Prison once housed some of Arizona's most notorious criminals. Courtesy of Rick Mortensen, Cincinnati.

threw the bloody mass into his face. Even if the crime didn't happen exactly that way, it's a pretty good rep to have behind bars.

New Cons on the Block

When new prisoners arrived at Yuma, they were assigned a number, their vital statistics were recorded, and they were photographed. A special mirror with a cutout placed on the shoulder was used so the photograph included a full face and profile view. The mirror is still on display at the park museum.

After a bath, male prisoners were issued a striped uniform, an extra pair of pants, a cap, two handkerchiefs, two pairs of socks, two pairs of underwear, one pair of shoes, a few sundries, and bedding. Then they would be escorted to a cell, which would be shared with five other men.

Three-tier bunk beds lined both sides of the narrow cell, 10 feet by 7 feet, with a chamber pot in the middle that served as a toilet. The beds were originally built of wood but were replaced with iron ones in 1901 to alleviate a severe bed-bug infestation.

Any prisoners who got out of line were subject to punishments that included solitary confinement, being fitted with a ball and chain, and getting tossed into the Dark Cell. Gouged out of the caliche hillside, the Dark Cell was a small room containing an iron cage. The only light streamed in through a ventilation shaft in the ceiling. Prisoners were stripped to their underwear, locked in the cage without even the luxury of a chamber pot, and given only bread and

---

Fast Fact: The Dark Cell was nicknamed the Snake Den. Stories circulated that the guards would drop snakes and scorpions down the ventilation shaft onto the prisoners, but there is no evidence that this actually happened.

---

water once a day. Often multiple prisoners shared the cage that was approximately 10 feet by 6 feet, and 5 feet tall. It was rarely cleaned, so the stench was overpowering. Welcome to the Yuma Pen.

Hellhole or Country Club?

While nothing about life behind bars seemed especially cushy, townsfolk were green with envy. Prisoners feared and loathed what they called the "Hellhole of the West." Yet plenty of Yuma residents, resenting how inmates were coddled at the place, nicknamed it the "Country Club on the Colorado."

The prison had amenities most Yuma homes did not, such as electricity, forced ventilation, and sanitation, including two bathtubs and three showers. There was even a prison library containing 2,000 books, making it the largest in the territory.

Work was mandatory for the prisoners. They made their own clothes, did construction in and around the prison, and farmed along the banks of the Colorado River. But there was seldom enough work to keep all the inmates occupied, as noted in an 1896 *Arizona Sentinel* article.

"One can go any day to the prison and see convicts singing and skylarking, joking, and all-in-all having a grand old time at the expense of the taxpayer. It is well known here that the prison on the hill is more a place of recreation and amusement than servitude."

When not busy "skylarking," prisoners could learn a trade, quite unusual for the penal system of its day. A school was also established, teaching prisoners to read and write, play music, or speak Spanish.

The Frail Prisoners

In a prison built for men, women caused all sorts of problems. Ultimately, 29 women, or "frail prisoners" as they were called, did time in Yuma. Although not much of it in

There's still an eerie quality to the Dark Cell at Yuma Prison.
Courtesy of Rick Mortensen, Cincinnati.

many cases. The first four female inmates arrived one at a time and were quickly pardoned by the governor because, with no other women to talk to, it seemed too much like solitary confinement.

Necessary accommodations were finally made to house females. The most infamous of those was stagecoach-robbing Pearl Hart. Others included Maria Moreno, who killed her brother with a shotgun because he did not like the way she was dancing. Rosie Duran and Elena Estrada were the only women to serve time in the Dark Cell, for fighting.

Manuela Fimbres was pregnant at the time of her incarceration and gave birth to a baby boy. The littlest yardbird stayed behind bars with his mother for the first

two years of his life until her release. Guards were not sorry to see the disagreeable Manuela go, but they sorely missed the youngster.

Hard Times

While the prison never ran out of cons, it did run out of real estate. Overcrowded conditions finally spelled the end of Yuma. Because it had no more room to expand, inmates were transferred to the new Florence Prison in 1909.

The Big House was suddenly empty. But not for long. From 1910 to 1914, the former hoosegow served as the local high school. When the football team traveled to Phoenix and beat the larger school, the opposing crowd taunted them with a chant of "Criminals." Yuma quickly embraced the name and the school has proudly been the home of the Criminals ever since.

In 1924 the Southern Pacific Railroad demolished the western end of Prison Hill to make way for new tracks. During the

Fast Fact: Of the 140 escape attempts from Yuma Prison, 26 were successful. Almost all were achieved by trusties working outside the prison walls.

Great Depression, hoboes riding the rails and homeless families lived in the cells.

Finally, in the early 1940s, Yuma residents came to the rescue to save what was left. Some restoration began and the prison was converted into a museum. It was donated to Arizona State Parks in 1960.

When the state parks faced their financial difficulties, partnerships forged with communities often kept the facilities open. Yuma stepped forward to save both its parks. Through fundraisers, donations, and the hard work of volunteers, the hilltop hoosegow was given an extensive makeover until it looked better than ever, although still gritty and authentic. It remains one of my favorite historic destinations. Today, visitors can walk through the sally port, the original 1876 adobe prison gateway. They can explore the granite cellblocks, climb into the guard tower, and feel the walls close in around them in the infamous Snake Den.

The museum building is filled with artifacts and exhibits including the Colt .45 Peacemaker belonging to Pearl Hart, leg irons, prisoner-made knives, the weight used to stretch the hangman's noose at the courthouse gallows, a Gatling gun like the one posted in the guard tower, uniforms, supplies, and a display of beautiful lace hand-knitted by a murderer in his spare time. The museum also has a great collection of photographs, vivid banners of mugshots adorning the walls, and an informative video that plays in the theater room. For those that would like a personalized memento, there's an inmate shirt on hand, along with cardboard strips of numbers, and the original mirror used by the cons. Kids and adults alike can pose for their own mug shot.

Before leaving, pay a visit to the prisoners left behind. No one was executed at Yuma, because capital punishment was administered by the county government. But 111 prisoners died while incarcerated, and 104 still lie in the sunbaked prison cemetery. It's a strange limbo for those poor unfortunates. The boneyard lies outside the prison walls, just above the river, but still in the shadow of the imposing guard tower. They escaped, yet it's probably not the eternal view they wanted.

CRIMES, MAYHEM, AND OTHER OUTRAGES

During the prison's 33 years of operation, 3,069 prisoners were incarcerated for a wide variety of crimes. Here are the crimes and the number of inmates sentenced for those crimes:

BURGLARY 1287
ASSAULT, MAYHEM, RIOT 473
FORGERY, FRAUD 249
MURDER 217
MANSLAUGHTER 170
SELLING LIQUOR TO INDIANS 164
ROBBERY 143
RAPE 42
ADULTERY 27
POLYGAMY 11
OBSTRUCTING RAILROAD 4
SEDUCTION 3
PRIZE FIGHTING 1

Pity the one poor sap nabbed for prizefighting. Courtesy of Rick Mortensen, Cincinnati.

When You Go

Yuma Territorial Prison State Historic Park is located at 220 North Prison Hill Road. It is open daily from 9:00 a.m. to 5:00 p.m. during the winter, but closed Tuesday and Wednesday from June 1 through September 30. 928-783-4771, azstateparks.com, www.yumaprison.org.

Admission

Adults and youths (7–13), $. Free admission for children 6 and under.

Events

Old West reenactment groups ride into Yuma every January for a series of epic shootouts. The prison makes an apt setting for the annual Gathering of the Gunfighters where the bodies will be stacked like cordwood. Figuratively, of course. Troupes perform elaborate skits and are judged on costumes, dialogue, character portrayal, use of weapons, stunts, entertainment value, and so on. It's a great show for the entire family.

AROUND TOWN

With more and more people wanting to know the origin of their food, the Yuma Visitors Bureau created the Field to Feast tours in 2011 in partnership with the University of Arizona Cooperative Extension. Field to Feast tours gives participants a chance to harvest fresh produce and eat a meal created from it just a couple of hours later. In between the field and the feast, visitors get a peek behind the scenes of Yuma's multibillion-dollar agricultural industry. Field to Feast tour dates run January through February.

Picnic Areas

A picnic area is located above the river with a nice view of California.

Visitor Center

Introductory exhibits, photos, and a gift shop with some cool prison-themed items are found at the visitor center.

Nearby Attractions

The Imperial National Wildlife Refuge, north of Yuma, harbors an intriguing mix of river, marshy wetlands, and backwater lakes bracketed by stark desert. The refuge was established to protect migratory birds and other wildlife along 30 miles of the lower Colorado River, including the last unchannelized section before the river enters Mexico. It's an especially bustling place in the winter when feathered visitors such as the cinnamon teal and northern pintail show up. During the milder seasons, Imperial National Wildlife Refuge offers birding tours, guided hikes, and stargazing events. 928-783-3371, www.fws.gov/refuge/imperial.

The Colorado River can be feisty in the upper canyons, but the Yuma portion is gentle and languid. Perfect for a leisurely float. Yuma River Tubing operates from April 1 through September 30. They provide tubes, coolers, and a ride upriver. You just drift back downstream to your starting point. Choose between three different floats, including a 1-mile happy-hour outing. An inflatable tube, a lazy river, and a warm day—what else in life do you need? 928-750-0247, www.yumarivertubing.com.

The University of Arizona Robert J. Moody Demonstration Garden is a sliver of serenity amid the bustle of town. It's designed to educate Yuma residents about gardening in the Southwest. All plants are labeled. A paved pathway weaves through the various plots, including the Children's Garden, the Healing Garden, and the Xeriscape Garden. Informational kiosks can be found throughout, and shaded benches and picnic tables invite quiet contemplation. Open during daylight hours. 2200 West 28th Street, 928-726-3904.

Acknowledgments

The author wishes to acknowledge the invaluable assistance of several people, most notably the members of Arizona State Parks and Trails, past and present—with very special thanks to Sue Black, Michelle Thompson, Ken "Gecko" Sliwa, Mickey Rogers, Sean Hammond, Monica Enriquez, Annette Johansen, Ellen Bilbrey, and Glenn Schlottman. Thanks to all the park rangers for their unwavering dedication to the job. A big shout-out to the hundreds of volunteers who do the work because they love the parks and who provide such a personal welcome to visitors from around the state and the world. Thanks to the communities, businesses, and sponsors who pitched in when the parks were struggling and kept the doors open and the lights on. Thanks to Rick Mortensen for spending some of his vacation days roaming around Arizona snapping photos for me. Thanks to Mike Koopsen for his great images and enthusiastic encouragement. Thanks always to Jill Cassidy for sending me to every corner of Arizona and for pretending not to notice when I turned in assignments late. And a very special thanks to my wife, Michele, who makes such a wonderful Arizona life possible.

Roger Naylor hiking at Dead Horse Ranch State Park.
Courtesy of Rick Mortensen, Cincinnati.

About the Author

Roger Naylor is an award-winning Arizona travel writer. He specializes in state and national parks, lonely hiking trails, twisting back roads, diners with burgers sizzling on the grill, small towns, ghost towns, and pie. In 2018 he was inducted into the Arizona Tourism Hall of Fame. His work has appeared in *Arizona Republic, USA Today, Go Escape, Arizona Highways, Western Art & Architecture*, and *Route 66 Magazine*. He is a senior writer for the Bob and Tom Show, a nationally syndicated radio program. He is the author of *The Amazing Kolb Brothers of Grand Canyon, Boots and Burgers: An Arizona Handbook for Hungry Hikers, Death Valley: Hottest Place on Earth*, and *Arizona Kicks on Route 66*. For more information, visit rogernaylor.com.

SOUTHWEST ADVENTURE SERIES
Ashley M. Biggers, Series Editor

The Southwest Adventure Series provides practical how-to guidebooks for readers seeking authentic outdoor and cultural excursions that highlight the unique landscapes of the American Southwest. Books in the series feature the best ecotourism adventures, world-class outdoor recreation sites, back-road points of interest, and culturally significant archaeological sites, as well as lead readers to the best sustainable accommodations and farm-to-table restaurants in Arizona, Colorado, Nevada, New Mexico, Utah, and Southern California.

Also available in the Southwest Adventure Series:

Eco-Travel New Mexico: 86 Natural Destinations, Green Hotels, and Sustainable Adventures by Ashley M. Biggers

Skiing New Mexico: A Guide to Snow Sports in the Land of Enchantment by Daniel Gibson